Study Guide

for Babbie's

# The Basics of Social Research
## Second Edition

**Theodore C. Wagenaar**
*Miami University*
*Oxford, Ohio*

**Earl Babbie**
*Chapman University*
*Orange, California*

**WADSWORTH**

**THOMSON LEARNING**

Australia • Canada • Mexico • Singapore • Spain • United Kingdom • United States

For more information, contact
**Wadsworth/Thomson Learning**
**10 Davis Drive**
**Belmont, CA 94002-3098**
**USA**

For more information about our products, contact us:
Thomson Learning Academic Resource Center
1-800-423-0563
http://www.wadsworth.com

**International Headquarters**
Thomson Learning
International Division
290 Harbor Drive, $2^{nd}$ Floor
Stamford, CT 06902-7477
USA

**UK/Europe/Middle East/South Africa**
Thomson Learning
Berkshire House
168-173 High Holborn
London WC1V 7AA
United Kingdom

**Asia**
Thomson Learning
60 Albert Complex, #15-01
Singapore 189969

**Canada**
Nelson Thomson Learning
1120 Birchmount Road
Toronto, Ontario M1K 5G4
Canada

ISBN 0-534-51906-7

# Contents

# Preface

This book is designed for use in conjunction with *The Basics of Social Research*, second edition, by Earl R. Babbie. Its purpose is to reinforce and extend your understanding of the information in the text and to provide opportunities for you to apply the material in the textbook.

Each chapter begins with objectives that focus your attention on the major points. They are specific statements of expected learning outcomes, and they will enhance your learning if you complete them. Glance through them before reading the chapter and refer to and complete them as you progress through the chapter. A summary follows. Reading the summary before and after reading the chapter will give you both a preview and a review of its contents.

A list of the key terms follows the summary. Mark each in the text and try to restate the definition in the text. Several of the definitions for these terms are presented in the matching exercises to give you some practice. The answers and page number references are contained in Appendix 2 for your convenience. The review questions test both knowledge and the ability to apply the concepts and principles presented in the text. Be sure to complete them and check your answers with the correct answers in Appendix 2. Page numbers are provided in the event you wish to determine why you answered a particular question incorrectly. Completing these questions will enhance your performance on exams.

The discussion questions encourage you to address several of the major issues raised in the chapter. Writing out the answers in your own words will strengthen your understanding and application of these issues.

The best way to learn research methods is through actual practice. Hence, we have included several short exercises for each chapter. Several of them involve you in analyzing data from the General Social Surveys by using SPSS, MicroCase, or another data analysis program. Before starting work on an exercise, we suggest you read through the entire exercise first so that you will know everything that is required. Reread those portions of the chapter that deal with the topics covered in the exercise. Then you should be ready to start work. In suggesting so many different exercises, it was our intention to provide you and your instructor with options. The exercises are all limited enough in scope that you will be able to complete many of them during the course. But we certainly did not intend for you to do them all. Make sure your instructor knows that. Instructors are reminded that suggested answers for some of the exercises are presented in the *Instructor's Manual*.

Comments and suggestions are welcome. Please address comments to Theodore C. Wagenaar, Miami University, Department of Sociology, Gerontology, and Anthropology, Oxford, OH 45056. Email: wagenatc@muohio.edu.

# Part 1

## An Introduction to Inquiry

1

# Chapter 1

## Human Inquiry and Science

## OBJECTIVES

1. Compare knowing things through agreement versus through experience.

2. Identify the two criteria needed for scientists to accept the reality of something they have not personally experienced.

3. Differentiate epistemology from methodology.

4. Define and illustrate causal reasoning and probabilistic reasoning.

5. Differentiate the scientific approach from the ordinary human inquiry approach to causal and probabilistic reasoning.

6. Differentiate prediction from understanding.

7. Describe the role of tradition and authority as sources of secondhand knowledge.

8. Define and illustrate each of the following errors in inquiry: inaccurate observations, overgeneralization, selective observation, and illogical reasoning.

9. Show how a scientific approach provides safeguards against each one of these errors.

10. Describe premodern, modern, and postmodern views of reality.

11. Describe the three major aspects of the overall scientific enterprise.

12. Define theory and indicate how it differs from philosophy or belief.

13. Give three examples of social regularities.

14. Define aggregate and present a rationale for why social scientists examine aggregates.

15. Give four examples of variables and their respective attributes.

16. Differentiate independent and dependent variables by definition and example, and show how they contribute to understanding causality.

17. Compare idiographic and nomothetic explanations.

18. Compare inductive and deductive theory.

19. Compare quantitative and qualitative data.

20. Differentiate pure from applied research.

## SUMMARY

People know what they know primarily through two processes. First, people know things through agreement, the things they consider to be real because they have been told they are real. Believing what we are told yields most of what we know. Second, people also know things through direct experience, primarily through observation. People have long struggled with determining what is real.

Science provides a way of looking at both agreement reality and experiential reality. The scientific approach to both realities demands that two criteria be met: an assertion must have both logical and empirical support. Hence science is a special form of human inquiry, the result of the human desire to predict future events and to understand patterns of cause and effect. The textbook will examine social science methodology, which could simply be called the science of finding out. Methodology is a sub-field of epistemology, the science of knowing.

Recognizing that some factors are caused by other factors lies at the root of ordinary human inquiry. That is, we use causal reasoning. Such patterns of cause and effect are probabilistic. That is, the cause usually but not always brings about the effect. Understanding ordinary human inquiry also means distinguishing prediction from understanding. While it is possible to predict something without necessarily understanding why it occurs, understanding usually yields improved prediction abilities. In short, ordinary human inquiry involves both what and why questions.

Tradition and authority comprise two important sources of agreement reality, our secondhand knowledge. Using tradition, we accept an inherited body of information and understanding. Tradition helps us avoid having to learn everything from scratch. Authority derives from the status of the transmitter of the knowledge. We tend to believe those with more credibility. But both authority and tradition can also hinder human inquiry.

Ordinary human inquiry is prone to several errors. First, casual observations are frequently inaccurate. Science helps alleviate this error by mandating conscious observation. Second, people frequently overgeneralize on the basis of a few limited observations. Scientists protect themselves against overgeneralization by employing large random samples and by replicating studies. Third, people observe selectively, by paying attention to events that match a prior conclusion and ignoring those that do not. The scientific approach helps protect against this error by specifying in advance the number and types of observations to be made and by having several scientists investigate the same phenomenon. A fourth error is illogical reasoning, such as using an exception to prove a rule. Science helps here by providing systems of logic. In comparison to casual inquiry, scientific inquiry is a conscious activity and is more careful than our casual inquiry.

Most people give little thought to the nature of reality, something philosophers refer to as "naive realism." The nature of "reality" is more complex than we tend to assume, and can be approached through three views of reality. The premodern view of reality played a key role in earlier civilizations and assumed that things really were the way humans saw them. The modern view considers differing views of reality as legitimate; there is no one best view of what is assumed to exist. The postmodern view holds that what is "real" simply reflects our points of view and that there is actually no "objective" reality to be observed. The postmodern view highlights the difficulty scientists have in observing and explaining what is "real" because scientists' personal orientations can affect what they observe and how they explain what they observe.

Science is based on logic and observation. The scientific enterprise involves theory, data collection, and data analysis. Theory meets the scientific criterion of logic by describing the logical relationships that exist among variables; it contributes to our understanding of what is observed. Data collection meets the scientific criterion of observation. Data analysis uncovers patterns in what is observed and helps compare what is logically expected with what is actually observed. Theory addresses what is, not what should be. Hence scientists cannot settle debates on values. In short, social science can only help in knowing what is and why.

Social scientific theory and research help uncover the social regularities underlying social life. Some people argue that contradictory cases negate social regularities; scientists point out that social regularities represent probabilistic patterns that need not apply to every situation. In short, social scientists analyze aggregates instead of individuals by examining the relationships between variables. They do so by examining the distributions of people across the attributes of variables that reflect causes (independent variables) and effects (dependent variables). Understanding causal connections remains paramount.

Four broad and connected distinctions underlie many of the variations of social research. The first involves two types of causal reasoning. Idiographic explanations address all or most of the unique factors that help explain one particular case. Nomothetic explanations, on the other hand, address the major factors that help explain something across many cases. Nomothetic explanations seek explanations with fewer causal variables and seek to explain the causal connection in a variety of cases.

The second distinction involves two types of theory. Inductive reasoning moves from particular observations to the discovery of a pattern underlying the particular observations. Deductive reasoning, on the other hand, moves from a pattern that might be logically or theoretically expected to observations that confirm or disconfirm the expected pattern.

The third distinction involves the difference between numerical and non-numerical data. Quantitative analysis helps make our observations more explicit and affords statistical analyses. Qualitative analysis provide greater detail and provide a greater richness of meaning than does quantitative analysis. The fourth distinction involves two motivations for scientists. Pure research seeks knowledge for knowledge's sake alone, while applied research seeks to apply knowledge to everyday problems in order to help address them.

## TERMS

1. aggregates
2. attributes
3. applied research
4. authority
5. causal reasoning
6. causation
7. data collection
8. data analysis
9. deductive theory
10. dependent variable
11. empiricism
12. epistemology
13. idiographic explanation
14. inaccurate observations
15. independent variable
16. inductive theory
17. methodology
18. modern view of reality
19. nomothetic explanation
20. overgeneralization
21. postmodern view of reality
22. prediction
23. premodern view of reality
24. probabilistic reasoning
25. pure research
26. qualitative data
27. quantitative data
28. relationship
29. selective observation
30. social regularities
31. theory
32. tradition
33. understanding
34. variables

## MATCHING

___ 1. The science of finding out.

___ 2. Explanation that seeks to identify the major factors that affect something across many cases.

___ 3. A source of knowledge that is obtained from experts.

___ 4. The assumption that a few similar events are evidence of a general pattern.

___ 5. Interpreting events to fit a general pattern that a researcher believes to be true.

___ 6. Logical and persistent patterns in social life.

___ 7. Logical groupings of attributes.

___  8.  An association that links variables.


## REVIEW QUESTIONS
(A reminder: the answers are in Appendix 2)

1.  Most of what we know is a matter of
    a. personal experience.
    b. a result of scientific discovery.
    c. empirical evidence.
    d. agreement reality.
    e. logical support.

2.  Which one of the following is the best example of agreement-based knowledge?
    a. you meet 15 Graskinos and conclude that they are all prejudiced
    b. you develop a scale to measure love and give it to 20 people
    c. you accept prejudice as wrong because that is what the Bible says
    d. you do not get right next to people when you talk to them because it violates a norm
    e. you run an experiment to test the effect of crowding

3.  The two foundations of science are
    a. tradition and observation.
    b. observation and logic.
    c. logic and theory.
    d. theory and observation.
    e. logic and generalization.

4.  When you hear the 4:27 train blow its whistle as you walk home from school every day, you can expect within minutes to smell Ms. Stockland's cooking. This is an example of
    a. understanding without prediction.
    b. understanding with prediction.
    c. prediction with understanding.
    d. prediction without understanding.
    e. scientific reasoning.

5.  "But my professor said that no significant differences exist between men and women regarding intelligence." What source of understanding does this example reflect?

a. personal experience
b. tradition
c. authority
d. public opinion
e. science

6.  A student meets two fraternity men at a party who talk about all the partying they do. She then concludes that all fraternity men party all the time. What error in understanding does this example reflect?
    a. inaccurate observation
    b. overgeneralization
    c. selective observation
    d. illogical reasoning
    e. overemphasis on authority

7.  In your discussion of measurement with a friend, she argues that what you are trying to measure does not exist and that your own point of view will determine what you perceive in your measuring process. She has taken which view of reality?
    a. correct
    b. premodern
    c. modern
    d. postmodern
    e. scientific

8.  You have just had a wonderful streak of great luck in your methods class: you've gotten A's on the last three tests and computer assignment. You have a research project due on the last day of class and you just know that you are going to flunk it. After all, something has to happen to break up this streak of good luck. You have fallen prey to the error of
    a. illogical reasoning.
    b. inaccurate observation.
    c. selective observation.
    d. over-emphasis on tradition.
    e. overgeneralization.

9.  Criminal justice student Vierling has noticed in her internship that adolescents who have experienced difficulties in school are more likely to become juvenile delinquents. In her process of going from specific observations to the discovery of a more general pattern, she has employed

a. social regularity thinking.
b. illogical reasoning.
c. deductive reasoning.
d. inductive reasoning.
e. nomothetic inquiry.

10. Science
    a. deals with what should be and ***not*** with what is.
    b. can settle debates on value.
    c. is exclusively descriptive.
    d. has to do with disproving philosophical beliefs.
    e. has to do with how things are and why.

11. Scientists do not study individuals per se, but instead study social patterns reflecting
    a. aggregates.
    b. collectivities.
    c. theories.
    d. attributes.
    e. norms.

12. Professor Fremming examined the following categories of marital status: married, never married, widowed, separated, and divorced. These categories are known as
    a. variables.
    b. attributes.
    c. variable categories.
    d. units of analysis.
    e. theoretical elements.

13. When social scientists study variables, they focus on
    a. attributes.
    b. groups.
    c. people.
    d. characteristics.
    e. relationships.

14. Senator Josephson researched the effects of political orientation on attitudes toward abortion. "Political orientation" is an example of
    a. an attribute.

      b. an independent variable.
      c. an aggregate.
      d. a unit of analysis.
      e. a dependent variable.

## DISCUSSION QUESTIONS

1. How do tradition and authority hinder inquiry?  How do they support it?  Give examples.

2. Present both sides of the argument that the scientific approach is the best approach to understanding.

3. Show how the three views of reality reflect the intellectual climate of the time during which they developed.

## EXERCISE 1.1                                    Name_____

Each of us is confronted with decisions in our everyday lives that require us to gather and assess information on the different alternatives at hand and then make a decision. Examples of such decisions include the decision to attend college, buy a car or some other item, strike up a friendship with Person A or B, select a particular course, or take a trip to Point X or Y. You may have made an error in such decisions because your information was flawed by one or more of the errors of human inquiry that Babbie describes, or the decision may have been correct but for some of the wrong reasons. Recall and describe a decision you have made that may have been flawed to some extent because information was based on one or more of the errors of human inquiry.

1.  Describe the decision.

2.  Identify which of the errors of human inquiry as described by Babbie were involved in this decision. Explain how each error was committed.

3.  Explain how a scientific approach would have helped reduce the effect of the error(s) of human inquiry in this decision.

# EXERCISE 1.2                          Name_____

List four social (not physical) regularities that are evident in day-to-day life. These could involve regularities in family life, friendship, large groups, work experiences, classroom activities, etc. Be sure you are describing social regularities. See the text for examples, but do not use these examples. Again, **avoid** physical examples.

## EXERCISE 1.3                                    Name_____

Variables and their attributes (or values) are at the heart of examining relationships in the social sciences. Key to formulating such relationships are independent and dependent variables. Select two relationships, each involving both an independent variable and a dependent variable. State each of the two relationships in a separate sentence. Each sentence should contain just two variables—an independent variable and a dependent variable—and should contain words which specify how the two variables are related to each other. The independent variable should be stated first in the sentence. You should then identify which is the independent variable and which is the dependent variable in each statement of a relationship. Explain why you expect there to be a relationship between the two variables. Then identify clearly the attributes of each variable.

Review the examples in the text if you have difficulty with this exercise. Be sure to use sociological variables and avoid those used in the text or by your instructor.

A few examples of incorrect and correct examples follow.

*Incorrect*: "Men like Fords better than Volvos." This is incorrect because there is only one variable, type of car liked. Men in this sentence is a constant, not a variable. *Correct*: "Men like cars more than women do." The independent variable is gender (attributes: male, female) and the dependent variable is liking cars (attributes: like much, like some, like little, etc.).

*Incorrect*: "High school graduates and college graduates hold jobs." This is incorrect because it really specifies a constant (holding jobs) that is associated with both attributes of the variable amount of education. *Correct*: "College graduates hold higher paying jobs than do high school graduates." The independent variable is amount of education (attributes: high school graduate, college graduate) and the dependent variable is amount of income (attributes: less than $5,000, $5,001-$10,000, etc.).

*Incorrect*: "Intelligence is related to grades." This statement does have two variables, but it is incorrect because the nature of the relationship is not specified. *Correct:* "The higher people's intelligence, the higher will be their grades." The independent variable is amount of intelligence (attributes: less than 70, 71-90, etc.) and the dependent variable is grades (attributes: A, B, etc.).

(continued)

1. For your first relationship, identify the independent and dependent variables, explain why you expect there to be a relationship, and describe the attributes of each. Remember to use sociological variables.

   a. The relationship:

   b. The independent variable:

   c. The dependent variable:

   d. Why you expect a relationship:

   e. The attributes of the independent variable:

   f. The attributes of the dependent variable:

(continued)

2.  For your second relationship, identify the independent and dependent variables, explain why you expect there to be a relationship, and describe the attributes of each. Remember to use sociological variables and do not use either of the two variables you used in #1.

    a. The relationship:

    b. The independent variable:

    c. The dependent variable:

    d. Why you expect a relationship:

    e. The attributes of the independent variable:

    f. The attributes of the dependent variable:

# EXERCISE 1.4                                    Name_____

Visit the Web site of the American Sociological Association (www.asanet.org). Click "Sociologists." Review the publicly available data sets described and select one (other than the General Social Survey) that interests you.

1.  Identity the data set you chose.

2.  Describe the aggregate(s) the data set examines.

3.  List three social regularities that could be examined with the data set.

4.  Identify a dependent variable that is or might be included in the data set and note two independent variables that may be connected to that dependent variable.

## EXERCISE 1.5                                    Name_____

Examine the variables reported in the General Social Survey, Appendix 1 in this volume. Identify five variables of interest, but pick those with relatively few attributes. Run a frequency distribution of these variables, using SPSS or MicroCase (or another data analysis program as indicated by your instructor).

1.  For each variable:
    a. list the variable
    b. describe the variable–see the label in Appendix 1
    c. list the attributes
    d. list the percentage in each attribute (use the valid percent column, the one with the missing values omitted from the percentage calculations)

2.  Select three of your variables and briefly summarize the distribution of cases across the attributes.

# EXERCISE 1.6                                    Name_____

Babbie discusses social scientists' desire to identify social regularities. One of those he mentions is that men earn more than women do. Use SPSS or MicroCase (or another data analysis program as indicated by your instructor) to test his observation by running a crosstabulation of income (REALINC3) by gender (SEX) (see Appendix 1). Be sure to put SEX on top (columns) and REALINC3 on the side (rows), and request column percentages.

1.  Show your table below.

2.  Interpret the results in terms of Babbie's observation.

# Chapter 2

## Paradigms, Theory, and Research

## OBJECTIVES

1. List the three functions of theory in research.

2. Define paradigm and describe their role in science.

3. Note the two benefits of knowing that we operate within a paradigm.

4. Differentiate macro-level theory from micro-level theory.

5. Provide synopses for each of the following paradigms: early positivism, conflict, symbolic interactionism, ethnomethodology, structural functionalism, feminist, and rational objectivity reconsidered.

6. Show the role of theory, operationalization, and observation in the traditional model of science.

7. Define hypothesis testing.

8. Differentiate inductive logic from deductive logic by definition and example.

9. Outline the steps in deductive theory construction.

21

## SUMMARY

Chapter 1 showed how scientific inquiry is a product of both logic and observation. Chapter 2 formalizes that analysis by examining the respective roles of theory and research. The close link between the two is again demonstrated.

It is risky to base research only on the observation of patterns. Social scientists use theory to provide logical explanations for observed patterns. Theory has three functions for social research. First, it helps prevent us from being taken in by flukes. Second, theories help us to make sense out of observed patterns and enable us to suggest other possibilities. Third, theories can shape and direct research efforts by suggesting likely discoveries through empirical observation.

Social scientists have used various frames of reference, known as paradigms, in their search for meaning. Paradigm usage helps us to better understand those operating under different paradigms. Paradigms also encourage us to move beyond our own favorite ones to others that shed a different light on what we wish to understand. The paradigms scientists employ helps determine which theories seem the most useful.

Paradigms often gain or lose popularity, but are seldom discarded completely. Different paradigms make different assumptions about the nature of social reality. Paradigms range from the macro level to the micro level. Macro-theory examines society at large or at least large portions of it, while micro-theory examines social life at the levels of individuals and small groups.

Many paradigms exist. Early positivism was founded by Comte, who was the first to suggest that society could be studied logically and rationally. His emphasis on positivism laid the foundation for the development of social science. The conflict paradigm suggests that conflict underlies much of social interaction. Conflict theorists have explored macro-level conflict (such as Marx's analysis of conflict among different economic classes) and micro-level conflict (such as Simmel's analysis of conflict within groups). Conflict theory illustrates how paradigms shape the kinds of observations we are likely to make, the facts we discover, and the conclusions we draw from those facts. Paradigms also influence our choice of relevant concepts.

Symbolic interactionists examine interactions among individuals and focus on how people gain a sense of self based on their interactions with others. They stress the use of language and symbols in their analyses.

Ethnomethodologists believe that people continually create social structure through their actions and interactions. By continually trying to make sense out of their lives, people create their own social realities. Violating social norms often helps us determine people's expectations and how they make sense of their world. Structural functionalism is based on the assumption that social systems are made up of various parts (structures), each of which contributes to the functioning of the whole social system. The feminist paradigm shows how gender differences relate to the rest of social organization. The analysis of the oppression of women in various societies has contributed to our understanding of oppression in general. The feminist paradigm questions the predominant views of social reality because such views have generally been developed by men.

Some scholars question the assumption of rationality underlying the growth in science and in the rise of bureaucratic structures. People do not always behave rationally. However, it is possible to study even nonrational behavior in a scientific manner. This approach also challenges the idea that scientists can really be as objective as the ideal image of science assumes. Postmodernists have questioned the belief that there is a logically-ordered, objective reality and that scientists can study it objectively. All human experiences, including those of scientists, are inescapably subjective.

There are three main elements in the traditional model of science: theory, operationalization, and observation. Theory provides a backdrop for clarifying possible relationships among variables. Operationalization enables the measurement of variables so that their relationships can be empirically examined. Observation involves the actual collection of data to test the hypothesized relationships. This entire strategy is also known as hypothesis testing.

Theory construction proceeds through deductive logic and/or inductive logic. With deductive logic, scientists progress from general principles and theories to specific cases. With inductive logic, they proceed from particular cases to more general theories. In reality, theory and research interact through a mix of both deduction and induction.

Deductive theory construction follows these major steps: (1) specify the topic of interest, (2) specify the range of phenomena the theory addresses, (3) identify and specify the major concepts and variables, (4) find out what is known about the relationships among the variables, and (5) reason logically from the propositions obtained in the preceding steps to the specific topic under analysis. The deductive approach underscores the two basic elements in science: logical integrity and empirical verification.

In contrast to the deductive approach, the inductive approach to theory construction strives to uncover patterns based on actual observation; this approach is also known as grounded theory. This approach is seen most often in field research, although it can be used in other designs as well. Grounded theorists argue that the inductive approach is superior to deductive theorizing because the social scientist does not enter the field with preconceived theoretical constraints.

The deductive and inductive approaches are two idealized logical models for linking theory and research. However, social scientists employ many variations on these two ideal models. Some studies, for example, display less connection between theory and research than do others.

Some people feel that theoretical and practical issues do not overlap. However, theory often provides the insight needed to both understand society and to change it.

## TERMS

1. conflict paradigm
2. deductive logic
3. ethnomethodology
4. feminist paradigm
5. grounded theory
6. hypothesis
7. hypothesis testing
8. inductive logic

9. macro-theory
10. micro-theory
11. operationalization
12. paradigm
13. structural functionalism
14. symbolic interactionism
15. theory

## MATCHING

___  1. The specification of the steps, procedures, or operations followed to actuallymeasure variables.

___  2. Reasoning from particular instances to generalizations.

___  3. A paradigm that examines interaction among individuals and how people gain a sense of self based on their interactions with others.

___  4. This paradigm shows how gender differences relate to the rest of social organization.

___  5.  This paradigm uses "methodology of the people" to examine how people continually create social structure through their actions and interactions.

___  6.  Reasoning from general principles and theories to specific cases.

___  7.  A general framework or viewpoint that organizes our view of something.

___  8.  The paradigm that focuses on how the components of society are interrelated.

## REVIEW QUESTIONS

1.  Professor Peters examined the gender makeup of politicians and then made conclusions about how the political institution reflects the other institutions of society. Which paradigm was she using?
    a.  ethnomethodology
    b.  post-positivism
    c.  role theory
    d.  feminist
    e.  exchange

2.  The three main elements of the traditional model of science are
    a.  theory, operationalization, observation.
    b.  operationalization, hypothesis testing, theory.
    c.  observation, experimentation, operationalization.
    d.  theory, observation, hypothesis testing.
    e.  experimentation, hypothesis testing, theory.

3.  Which of the following is the *best* example of a hypothesis?
    a.  The greater the level of education, the greater the tolerance for alternative lifestyles.
    b.  Socialization in childhood has a significant impact on adolescent gender-role identity.
    c.  There are more female than male college students.
    d.  Religiosity equals frequency of church attendance and praying.
    e.  Actions are based on perceived costs and rewards.

4.  Which of the following is the *best* example of macro-level theory?
    a.  a study of play interactions among children

     b. a study of arguments among friends

     c. a study of cheating among students

     d. a study of the role of corporate mergers in the global economy

     e. a study of tax audits conducted by the IRS

5. Professor Pellson noticed that the students who sat in the front row in her classes usually got A's. After observing this pattern over several semesters, she decided that students who sit in the front row are generally good students. This is an example of

     a. deductive reasoning.

     b. inductive reasoning.

     c. probabilistic reasoning.

     d. causal reasoning.

     e. deterministic reasoning.

6. Babbie reviews the traditional model for portraying science. This model shows that science

     a. generally begins with theories.

     b. generally begins with hypotheses.

     c. generally begins with observations.

     d. generally begins with empirical conclusions.

     e. generally begins with measurement.

7. Whose emphasis on positivism laid the foundation for the development of social science?

     a. Weber

     b. Darwin

     c. Comte

     d. Garfinkel

     e. Mead

8. Professor Havidan studied a prenatal class for expectant parents in his attempt to understand how expectant parents prepare for the role of parenthood and how they gain a sense of themselves as parents. He focused on the language and symbols expectant parents use to describe their new roles. Which paradigm is he using?

     a. role theory

     b. feminist

     c. ethnomethodology

     d. structural functionalism

e. symbolic interactionism

9. Deductive theory construction generally begins with
    a. specifying topic of interest.
    b. specifying the range of phenomena the theory addresses.
    c. identifying and specifying the major concepts and variables.
    d. finding out what is known about the hypothesized relationships.
    e. reasoning logically from the propositions obtained to the specific topic under analysis.

10. The inductive approach to theory construction is seen most often in
    a. survey research.
    b. experimental research.
    c. field research.
    d. use of available data.
    e. content analysis.

11. The paradigm that accounts for the impact of economic conditions on family structures is
    a. symbolic interactionism.
    b. structural functionalism.
    c. positivism.
    d. conflict.
    e. exchange.

12. Which of the following is *not* a step in deductive theory construction? Or are they all steps?
    a. specify the topic
    b. identify the major concepts and variables
    c. identify propositions about the relationships among those variables
    d. reason logically from those propositions to the specific topic one is examining
    e. all are steps

13. Professor Todd observes playground interaction for a month to develop a theory that accounts for the problems observed. This is an example of
    a. deductive theorizing.
    b. grounded theory.
    c. conceptualization.
    d. ex post facto hypothesizing.
    e. paradigm estimation.

## DISCUSSION QUESTIONS

1. Babbie discusses several paradigms: early positivism, conflict, symbolic interactionism, ethnomethodology, structural functionalism, and the feminist paradigm. Briefly summarize each of these, as well as his points on rational objectivity reconsidered. Then select one topic of interest and show how three of the paradigms would examine that topic.

2. Figure 2-2 in the text portrays the traditional image of science. Describe that model, being certain to discuss the role of the three main elements: theory, operationalization, and observation.

3. Describe how the elements of theory construction fit together. Be specific.

4. Contrast deductive and inductive logic. Describe specific research issues that are appropriate for each and explain why.

5. Show how theory and research are closely linked. Indicate what each contributes to the other.

## EXERCISE 2.1                                Name_____

A major focus of this chapter is the difference between deductive and inductive logic. Your assignment is to develop studies using each approach.

### DEDUCTIVE LOGIC

1. Identify a topic of interest. You might select religiosity, feminism, or occupational success if you cannot identify a topic.

2. Explain what your theory will address. It might be factors promoting religiosity, why some people are more feminist than others, or why some people are more successful in their occupations than others.

3. Specify the range of phenomena your theory addresses. All people? Women only? Americans only?

(continued)

4.  Identify and specify your major concepts and variables. Don't just list your major concepts and variables, but actually develop and state your theory. Your theory does not have to be very complex. Keep in mind that a theory is an explanation of the causes of some phenomenon. Your theory may have one or more statements in it.

5.  Derive at least one specific testable hypothesis, such as: younger females are more likely to be feminist than older females. Be sure your hypothesis reflects a specific relationship between two variables.

(continued)

**INDUCTIVE LOGIC**

1.  Select one of the following "observations" or select one of your own. If you
    select one of your own, make sure it is very specific.
    a. women like coed residence halls more than men do
    b. students prefer male instructors over female instructors
    c. older people are more likely to vote Republican than are younger people
    d. your own:


2.  Describe the specific behaviors or statements made by people that might lead to
    the observation you selected.




3.  Based on the discussions and examples in the chapter, derive (make up) a reason-
    able theory for your observation. It should be more general than your observa-
    tion.

# EXERCISE 2.2                                   Name_____

Babbie describes the major social scientific paradigms. Identify and briefly summarize three major paradigms in one of the other disciplines you have encountered in college. Examples of disciplines include history, political science, economics, and psychology. Please note that the paradigms you describe will most likely be different from those discussed in the text; you need to identify the paradigms appropriate to the particular discipline you choose. Explain your choice of discipline and paradigms.

Discipline:

Paradigm # 1:

Paradigm # 2:

Paradigm # 3:

## EXERCISE 2.3                     Name_____

Imagine that you are a social scientist who wishes to examine in greater detail the implications of the paradigms discussed by Babbie. Specifically, you wish to apply the conflict and the structural functionalism paradigms in a study of how your school works. Give examples of how each paradigm may affect what you examine in your study.

Conflict paradigm:

Structural functionalism paradigm:

## EXERCISE 2.4
Name_____

Use one of the Web search engines to locate additional information on one of the theoretical paradigms Babbie discusses (see www.socsciresearch.com for a guide to sociology sites). Or visit Michael Kearl's Sociological Tour of Cyberspace for some sites on theory (www.trinity.edu/~mkearl/index.html).

1. Identify the paradigm you selected.

2. Note two additional conclusions you can make about this paradigm that either amplify points raised in the text or raise new points about this paradigm.

# EXERCISE 2.5

Name_____

Review Babbie's analysis of the conflict paradigm. Using deductive theory construction, we could hypothesize that more successful people will be most satisfied with the way things are because they benefit more from current social arrangements. Use SPSS or MicroCase (or another data analysis program as indicated by your instructor) to test this observation by running a crosstabulation of HAPPY by PRESTIG3 (see Appendix 1). Be sure to put PRESTIG3 on top (columns) and HAPPY on the side (rows), and request column percentages.

1. Present your table.

2. Analyze the percentage differences to determine if the hypothesis is correct.

# Chapter 3

## The Ethics and Politics
## of Social Research

## OBJECTIVES

1. Discuss why ethical issues are frequently not apparent to the researcher.

2. Describe and illustrate the ethical issues involved in the following: voluntary participation, no harm to subjects, anonymity and confidentiality, the researcher's identity, and analysis and reporting.

3. Describe the role of Institutional Review Boards.

4. Identify which of the ethical principles were violated in the Humphreys tearoom study.

5. Identify which of the ethical principles were violated in the Milgram shock study.

6. Describe two ways in which ethical and political concerns differ.

7. Summarize the link between objectivity and ideology.

8. Compare the positions on the issue that social science can (or cannot) and should (or should not) be separated from politics.

9. Illustrate how political issues exist in some of the research on race relations.

10.  Identify the political issues in Project Camelot.

11.  Identify the three main purposes of Babbie's discussion on politics.


## SUMMARY

Thus far the text has dealt with scientific and administrative constraints on practicing social research. The importance of workable compromises has been addressed. But practicing social research involves two other important considerations: ethics and politics. Social scientists often disagree on ethical and political questions because many such issues are not always immediately apparent, and few present clear and absolute solutions.

Social scientists generally agree on five basic principles in handling ethical concerns. Voluntary participation is the first principle. This principle is important because social research often represents an intrusion into people's lives and often requires that people reveal personal information about themselves. Social research often requires that people reveal such information to strangers—the researchers. Although other professionals such as physicians and lawyers also require such information and are strangers to the person, the social researcher cannot make the claim that revealing information is required to serve the personal interests of the respondent. But social scientists do argue that involvement in research may ultimately help all humanity.

Some research subjects such as students and prisoners believe that participation might benefit them personally, and in such situations the decision to participate may not be purely voluntary. A different problem is presented by the scientific norm of generalizability, which requires that research findings should be based on representative samples. Voluntary participation compromises this principle.

Social scientists should never injure participants, regardless of whether or not participants volunteered for the study. This second principle pertains primarily to psychological harm, which may result from asking people to reveal deviant behavior, unpopular attitudes, demeaning personal characteristics, and the like. This principle also applies when participants are asked to deal with aspects of themselves that they do not normally consider, a practice that may cause some agony. Subjects may also be harmed by the reporting of data, such as when recognition is possible. Increasingly, federal and other funding agencies require an independent evaluation of the treatment of human subjects, which may help the researcher identify inappropriate research strategies.

The third principle involves protecting the anonymity and confidentiality of research subjects. This principle is related to the previous one of protecting the subject from harm. A respondent is anonymous when the researcher cannot connect a given response with a given respondent. In a confidential study, the researcher is able to identify a given person's responses but promises not to reveal this identity. Confidentiality can be enhanced by using identification numbers instead of names.

Fourth, the researcher's identity can also be an ethical problem. Often it is useful and even necessary to identify oneself as a researcher. Other times it is possible and important to conceal one's research identity. Doing so may enhance the completeness and accuracy of the data collected. But doing so also involves a serious ethical dilemma since deceiving people is generally unethical. Social scientists sometimes handle this dilemma by identifying themselves as researchers but failing to inform the respondent of the true nature of the study, which also poses an ethical dilemma. It is important to debrief subjects after the study to minimize the effects of deception.

Fifth, ethical concerns enter in the analysis and reporting of data. Ethical obligations to colleagues dictate accurate reporting of the shortcomings and negative findings in a study. Also, social scientists should not identify accidental findings as the product of careful hypothesizing and theorizing.

Federal law affects ethical issues in social research. Any agency which receives federal research support must create an "Institutional Review Board." This board includes faculty (and sometimes other professionals) who review research proposals involving human subjects to insure that the subjects' rights and interests are being protected. In addition, most social science professional associations have created and published formal codes of ethics.

Two studies have gained notoriety for the ethical issues they have raised: Laud Humphreys's participant observation study of homosexuality in public restrooms and Stanley Milgram's laboratory studies of obedience to authority. Humphreys's work has been attacked by people both within and outside the social scientific community for his invasion of the privacy of the homosexuals and for his deceit in obtaining their identities. Milgram's shock experiments have been criticized for the psychological suffering experienced by the participants.

Ethical issues are distinguished from political issues in two respects. The ethics of social research apply more to the methods employed, and political issues are more concerned with the substance and use of research. Second, there are no formal codes of acceptable political conduct comparable to the codes of ethical conduct that many professional associations have established.

One exception to the absence of political norms is the generally accepted stance that a researcher's personal political orientation should not influence the research completed or the interpretations of such research. This agreement enhances objectivity by means of intersubjectivity, whereby social scientists with different subjective views arrive at the same results when they apply the same techniques. However, this notion of "value-free sociology" has come under attack in recent years as Marxist and neo-Marxist researchers have argued that social science should be clearly linked to social action. They argue that explanations of the current state of affairs inevitably results in defending the status quo.

There are numerous examples of social research intertwined with politics. Social scientific research has influenced American racial policies and has generated political and ideological debates within the social science community. Project Camelot was designed to assess the causes of war and to identify the actions a government could take to preclude such wars. Many social scientists argue that such a study would involve using social scientific research to strengthen established governments and to thwart revolutionary movements. The project was canceled as the Defense Department came under increasing attack for attempting to subvert social research.

In short, social science research is closely connected with political concerns. But it is also clear that social science research proceeds even under political controversy and hostility. It is also important to make ideological considerations a part of the backdrops we create, which will improve our awareness as we study research methods.

## TERMS

1. anonymity
2. code of ethics
3. confidentiality
4. debriefing
5. Institutional Review Boards
6. Project Camelot
7. value-free sociology
8. voluntary participation

## MATCHING

___  1.  An ethical principle that presupposes the willingness of respondents to participate in social research.

___  2.  The condition that exists when the researcher cannot identify a given response with a given respondent.

___  3.  The condition that exists when the researcher is able to identify a given person's responses but promises not to do so publicly.

___  4.  Published formal guidelines for conducting social research.

___  5.  Sociology that is relatively unaffected by personal values.

___  6.  A study that showed that ultimately science is neutral on such subjects as peace and war but that individual scientists are not.

## REVIEW QUESTIONS

1.  Ethical considerations enter at which point in the research process?
    a. selection of topic
    b. selection of subjects
    c. data gathering
    d. data analysis
    e. at all stages

2.  Ethics are *not* a consideration in which one of the following fields of research? Or do ethics enter in all of these fields?
    a. natural sciences
    b. psychology
    c. medical
    d. sociology
    e. ethics enter in all of them

3.  The *major* justification the social scientist has for requesting participation in a study is that
    a. it may help the respondent.

b. it may help all humanity.

c. it may help the social scientist.

d. it may help government officials make policy decisions.

e. it may help improve the educational system.

4. The ethical principle of voluntary participation *most* threatens which scientific goal?

   a. parsimony

   b. objectivity

   c. cumulativeness

   d. generalizability

   e. intersubjectivity

5. For her senior project in political science, Cheri conducts a survey on students' attitudes and behavior concerning homosexuality. While distributing the questionnaire, she assures the group of students that no one will be able to trace responses to an individual. However, she has obtained a seating chart with the names of all the students in the class and where they were sitting. Cheri is violating which ethical principle?

   a. confidentiality

   b. anonymity

   c. harm to subjects

   d. concealed identity of researcher

   e. voluntary participation

6. The controversy surrounding Milgram's study involving "shocks" suggests he *most* violated which ethical principles?

   a. harm to subjects and concealed purpose of study

   b. anonymity and harm to subjects

   c. confidentiality and harm to subjects

   d. concealed purpose of study and anonymity

   e. concealed purpose of study and confidentiality

7. The controversy surrounding Laud Humphreys's study of homosexuals suggests he *most* violated which of the following ethical principles?

   a. anonymity and confidentiality

   b. harm to subjects and data reporting without identification

   c. concealed identity of researcher and anonymity

   d. value-free inquiry and concealed identity of researcher

   e. harm to subjects and anonymity

8.  What is considered ethical is based on
    a. a list of moral absolutes.
    b. the authority of the state.
    c. agreed upon principles within a community.
    d. cultural directives.
    e. codes of political behavior.

9.  Federally mandated human subjects committees in universities were designed *primarily* to address which one of the following ethical principles?
    a. no harm to participants
    b. confidentiality
    c. anonymity
    d. voluntary participation
    e. identification of research purpose

10. Which of the following is *not* a difference between ethical and political aspects of social research? Or are they all differences?
    a. Ethical considerations are more objective than political considerations.
    b. Ethical aspects include a professional code of ethics, whereas political aspects do not.
    c. Ethics deal more with methods, whereas political issues deal with substance.
    d. Ethical norms have been established, whereas political norms, for the most part, have not been established.
    e. All are differences.

11. Recently, Marxist scholars have argued that social research should be closely connected to social action. Which feature of science is *most* threatened by this position?
    a. intersubjectivity
    b. objectivity
    c. parsimony
    d. cumulativeness
    e. generalizability

12. The concern with Project Camelot on internal war focused on
    a. the principle of voluntary participation.
    b. the principle of anonymity.
    c. the role of social scientists in helping defuse revolutions.
    d. the role of social scientists in helping obtain more money for defense purposes.
    e. the principle of political ideology.

## DISCUSSION QUESTIONS

1.  Summarize the ethical agreements discussed in the text. Which one do you think is the most important? Why?

2.  Discuss which of the ethical agreements were violated in the Humphreys study of homosexuality and in the Milgram study of obedience.

3.  Discuss the similarities and differences between the political and ethical aspects of social science research.

# EXERCISE 3.1                    Name_____

Listed below are research situations that involve ethics. You are to rank order these situations in terms of how seriously they violate the ethical agreements discussed in the chapter and to explain the reasons for your rankings.

a.  A psychology instructor asks students in an introductory class to complete questionnaires that the instructor will analyze and use in preparing a journal article for publication.

b.  After a field study of deviant behavior during a riot, law enforcement officials demand that the researcher identify those persons who were observed looting. Rather than risk arrest as an accomplice after the fact, the researcher complies.

c.  After completing the final draft of a book reporting a research project, the author discovers that 25 of the 2,000 survey interviews were falsified by interviewers but chooses to ignore that fact and publish the book anyway.

d.  A Ph.D. candidate gains access to an underground mine as a researcher-employee by telling management that he has a BA degree and wants to get some practical experience before going on for a degree in metallic engineering. He is very familiar with mining work.

e.  A college instructor wants to test the effect of unfair berating on exam performance. She administers an exam to both sections of a course. The overall performance of the two sections is essentially the same. The grades of one section are artificially lowered and the instructor berates the students for performing so badly. She then administers the same final exam to both sections and discovers that the performance of the unfairly berated section is worse. The hypothesis is confirmed, and the results are published.

f.  In a study of sexual behavior, the investigator wants to overcome subjects' reluctance to report what they might regard as deviant behavior. To get past their reluctance, subjects are asked, "Everyone masturbates now and then; about how often do you masturbate?"

g.  A researcher discovers that 85 percent of students smoke marijuana regularly at a school. Publication of this finding will probably create a furor in the community. Because no extensive analysis of drug use is planned, the researcher decides to ignore the finding and keep it quiet.

(continued)

h.  To test the extent to which people may try to save face by expressing attitudes on matters they are wholly uninformed about, the researcher asks for their attitudes regarding a fictitious issue.

i.  A research questionnaire is circulated among students as part of their university registration packet. Although students are not told they must complete the questionnaire, the hope is that they will believe they must, thereby ensuring a higher completion rate.

j.  A researcher promises participants in a study a summary of the results. Later, due to a budget cut, the summary is not sent out.

k.  A professor rewrites a thesis of one of his or her graduate students into an article and lists himself/herself as the sole author.

l.  A panel of reputable social scientists is pressing for Congressional approval of a National Data Service, which would combine all data on particular individuals from separate data files into one master data file. The advantages of such a center would be reduced duplicity of efforts and an increased number of variables per individual.

m.  A graduate student joins an Internet discussion board about the sports car that she drives. She occasionally posts some responses on the board and decides to do a sociological study about the sense of community experienced by members. She attends a car rally sponsored by the board and mingles with participants. She uses archived discussion posts and notes she kept while at car rallies for her study.

---

1.  For each of the above issues, identify what you believe to be the one or two ethical principles that are most apparent in the situation. Explain why.

    a:

    b:

    c:

    d:

(continued)

e:

f:

g:

h:

i:

j:

k:

l:

m:

2.  Place each situation in one of the following three groups:

|         Minor ethical | Moderate ethical | Severe ethical |
|         violations | violations | violations |

3.  Explain the criteria that you used in your rankings.

## EXERCISE 3.2                    Name_____

Listed below are some goals and techniques associated with "ethical" social science research. Describe briefly how each might conflict with one or more of the "scientific" norms of social research discussed in the first few chapters. Use real or hypothetical research examples to illustrate your answers. For each ethical norm be sure to describe a specific scientific norm that it would conflict with, and be sure to present a real or hypothetical example of how each conflict might occur and what the conflict would be about. Also, for each conflict, indicate which norm—the ethical or the scientific—you would decide to go along with and explain why you made the decision you did.

1. Voluntary participation.
   a. How it conflicts with a scientific norm:


   b. Example of conflict:


   c. Which norm you would follow and why:



2. Anonymity and confidentiality.
   a. How it conflicts with a scientific norm:


   b. Example of conflict:


   c. Which norm you would follow and why:


(continued)

3.  No harm to subjects.
    a.  How it conflicts with a scientific norm:



    b.  Example of conflict:



    c.  Which norm you would follow and why:




4.  Identifying yourself as a researcher.
    a.  How it conflicts with a scientific norm:



    b.  Example of conflict:



    c.  Which norm you would follow and why:




5.  Identifying the sponsor of your research.
    a.  How it conflicts with a scientific norm:



    b.  Example of conflict:



    c.  Which norm you would follow and why:

## EXERCISE 3.3                           Name_____

Visit the Web site of the American Sociological Association (www.asanet.org, click "sociologists") or the site for the British Sociological Association (www.britsoc.org.uk/about/ethic.htm) and review the code of ethics.

1. Cite the language that addresses each of the ethical issues Babbie addresses: voluntary participation, no harm to subjects, anonymity and confidentiality, the researcher's identity, and analysis and reporting.

2. Summarize the code's content about the politics of social research.

3. Identify three other topics addressed in the code and summarize the content.

# EXERCISE 3.4                    Name_____

Review the General Social Survey in Appendix 1, including the introduction. Determine how adequately this study addresses each of the ethical issues Babbie addresses: voluntary participation, no harm to subjects, anonymity and confidentiality, the researcher's identity, and analysis and reporting.

1. Voluntary participation.

2. No harm to subjects.

3. Anonymity and confidentiality.

4. Researcher identity.

5. Analysis and reporting.

# Part 2

## The Structuring of Inquiry

# Chapter 4

## Research Design

## OBJECTIVES

1.  Identify the two major aspects of research design.

2.  Define and illustrate the three basic purposes of research.

3.  List three reasons for performing exploratory studies.

4.  Describe the three main criteria for nomothetic, causal relationships.

5.  Describe the three false criteria for nomothetic causation.

6.  Differentiate necessary and sufficient causes.

7.  Define units of analysis and identify and illustrate each of the basic types.

8.  Define and illustrate the ecological fallacy.

9.  Define and illustrate reductionism.

10. Select four possible research issues, and identify the unit of analysis for each.

11. Compare cross-sectional and longitudinal studies in terms of the advantages and weaknesses of each.

12. Differentiate among the three types of longitudinal studies–trend, cohort, and panel–by definition and example.

13. Explain how longitudinal studies may be approximated using the cross-sectional design

14. Depict the research process in a diagram and describe the diagram.

15. Identify the basic elements of a research proposal.

## SUMMARY

Research design involves developing strategies for executing scientific inquiry. It involves specifying precisely what you want to find out and determining the most efficient and effective strategies for doing so. Appropriate research designs enable the social scientist to make observations and interpret the results.

Social scientists typically have one or more of the following as goals for their research: exploration, description, and explanation. Exploratory studies are often done when a researcher is examining a new interest, or when the subject of study is relatively uncharted. They help to determine the feasibility of a larger scale study and to develop the methods for such a study. The researcher's intent in a descriptive study is to observe and describe some segment of social reality. Explanatory studies are undertaken to identify possible causal variables of a given social phenomenon, thereby contributing to understanding.

Recall that nomothetic explanations identify a few factors (independent variables) that can explain much of the variation in a particular dependent variable. There are three main criteria for establishing nomothetic, causal relationships in social science research. First, there must be a correlation between the two variables. That is, as the independent variable changes, the dependent variable changes. Second, the time order must be clear: the independent variable must come before the dependent variable. Third, the relationship must be non-spurious. That is, the observed relationship between the independent and dependent variables cannot result from the impact of a third variable.

Three caveats apply to these criteria. First, social scientists speak in terms of probablistic causation, not complete causation. That is, a pattern exists, but that pattern does not apply to everyone studied. Second, exceptions to the pattern do not disprove a causal relationship. Third, we focus on relative differences. That is, we compare the categories of the variables to see if there is a difference, even though all the categories may show relatively low or high scores.

Knowing about necessary and sufficient causes may help us better understand false criteria for causality. A necessary cause represents a condition that must be present for the effect to follow. A sufficient cause represents a condition that, if it is present, guarantees the effect in question. Note that a sufficient cause is not the only possible cause of a particular effect. Note also that a cause can be sufficient, but not necessary. In the social sciences we never discover single causes that are absolutely necessary and absolutely sufficient when analyzing the nomothetic relationships among variables. However, we do occasionally find causal factors that are either 100-percent necessary or 100-percent sufficient. Idiographic causes are sufficient but not necessary.

Social scientists typically study individual people as their units of analysis, although they do so in aggregate form. But they also frequently study social groups, such as families. Even though the unit of analysis is the group, characteristics of the group may be derived from the characteristics of individual members. Formal social organizations, like a corporation, are also a unit of analysis. Finally, social artifacts are the products of social beings or their behavior and can also be analyzed. It is critically important to identify the units of analysis in a study accurately. Failure to do so may result in committing the ecological fallacy: gathering data on one unit of analysis but making assertions regarding another. Reductionism is another type of faulty reasoning connected to units of analysis. Reductionism involves using a single, narrow concept or set of concepts to explain complex phenomena.

Another aspect of research design is the time dimension. The major distinction lies between cross-sectional studies (observations at one point in time) and longitudinal studies (observations made at multiple time points). There are three types of longitudinal studies. Trend studies are those that examine changes within a population over time. Cohort studies examine more specific subpopulations as they change over time.

Panel studies examine the same set of people over time. Longitudinal studies are clearly superior for making causal assertions, but approximations to this design are frequently found in cross-sectional studies through such techniques as using simple logic, establishing clarity of time order of the variables, asking retrospective questions, and making age-cohort comparisons.

In short, the research process begins with an interest, idea, or theory, which in turn mandates clear conceptualization and operationalization. Appropriate research designs and sampling strategies must be used. The product is a series of observations, which are processed and analyzed, and the results are linked with the original framework of the study. Potential applications of the results should be considered. Although the research process does not always proceed in such a neat fashion, all these elements must be addressed. In designing a research project, researchers find it useful to assess their own interests, their abilities, and the resources available. Some find that multiple research strategies are the most effective, a process known as triangulation.

Research proposals are used to describe a potential study explicitly. They involve a clear statement of the problem, a literature review, a description of the subjects, a description of the measurement and data collection methods, an outline of the intended analyses, a schedule, and a budget.

## TERMS

1.  cohort studies
2.  cross-sectional studies
3.  description
4.  ecological fallacy
5.  explanation
6.  exploration
7.  idiographic explanation
8.  longitudinal studies
9.  necessary cause
10. nomothetic explanation
11. panel studies
12. reductionism
13. social artifacts
14. sufficient cause
15. trend studies
16. units of analysis

## MATCHING

___ 1.  Explaining complex phenomena in terms of a single, narrow concept or set of concepts.

___ 2. The purpose of research that stresses the determination of causes.

___ 3. The "what" or "whom" that is actually studied.

___ 4. The error in which data are gathered from one unit of analysis but conclusions are made about another unit of analysis.

___ 5. The purpose of research that stresses examining a new area of interest or studying uncharted areas.

___ 6. Studies in which the units of analysis are studied at one point in time.

___ 7. Longitudinal studies in which independent samples of the same age group are studied at two points in time or more.

___ 8. Longitudinal studies in which the same sample is studied at two points in time or more.

## REVIEW QUESTIONS

1. Exploratory studies are done most often for purposes of
   a. predicting future behavior, testing feasibility of a more careful study, developing methods to be used in a more careful study.
   b. connecting empirical reality with theory, satisfying a researcher's curiosity, developing methods to be used in a more careful study.
   c. satisfying a researcher's curiosity, testing feasibility of a more careful study, developing methods to be used in a more careful study.
   d. connecting empirical reality with theory, predicting future behavior, developing methods to be used in a more careful study.
   e. satisfying a researcher's curiosity, testing feasibility of a more careful study, connecting empirical reality with theory.

2. The degree of relationship between two variables is of particular concern in which type of study?
   a. exploratory
   b. descriptive
   c. explanatory
   d. qualitative
   e. panel

3.  Researcher Lewis spends three months as a choir member touring Europe to see what off-stage choir member interaction is all about. This is an example of which kind of study?
    a. cohort
    b. cross-sectional
    c. exploratory
    d. descriptive
    e. trend

4.  Professor Johannison has just discovered that amount of time spent in social activities has a causal influence on academic performance. This is an example of which kind of study?
    a. explanatory
    b. exploratory
    c. cross-sectional
    d. descriptive
    e. trend

5.  If a researcher wanted to find out how much time elderly persons in nursing homes spend interacting with each other, the researcher would conduct which kind of study?
    a. exploratory
    b. cohort
    c. explanatory
    d. descriptive
    e. time-lag

6.  Which of the following *best* reflects the ecological fallacy?
    a. data gathered from individuals, conclusions drawn about individuals
    b. data gathered from individuals, conclusions drawn about groups
    c. data gathered from groups, conclusions drawn about organizations
    d. data gathered from groups, conclusions drawn about individuals
    e. data gathered from organizations, conclusions drawn about nations

7.  Read the following statement and then determine the appropriate unit of analysis: "most Americans believe in God." What unit of analysis is reflected?
    a. individual
    b. group
    c. organization
    d. artifact
    e. collective

8.  Read the following statement and then determine the appropriate unit of analysis: "ten percent of families in a community move within a year." What unit of analysis is reflected?
    a. individual
    b. group
    c. organization
    d. artifact
    e. collective

9.  Read the following statement and then determine the appropriate unit of analysis: "church records show that contributions have declined over the past 20 years." What unit of analysis is reflected?
    a. individual
    b. group
    c. organization
    d. artifact
    e. collective

10. A particular weakness in cross-sectional studies is that
    a. too often too few people are studied.
    b. too often too few variables are studied.
    c. they are limited to individuals as the units of analysis.
    d. they are too descriptive and insufficiently explanatory.
    e. they make it difficult to infer causality.

11. Professor Lodwicky used the 1990 United States Census and the 1980 Census to compare the average family size. This reflects which type of study?
    a. cross-sectional exploratory
    b. cross-sectional descriptive
    c. trend exploratory
    d. trend descriptive
    e. panel exploratory

12. Which type of study would *best* enable a researcher to assess changes associated with attending college for four years?
    a. cross-sectional
    b. longitudinal
    c. trend
    d. cohort
    e. panel

13. Which one of the following is *not* an appropriate strategy for approximating longitudinal studies when only cross-sectional data are available?
    a. using logical inference
    b. examining the time order of the variables
    c. examining differences in responses of those who return their questionnaires early versus late
    d. examining age differences
    e. asking respondents to recall their pasts

14. The research proposal generally begins with
    a. a literature review.
    b. a statement of a problem or objective.
    c. identifying subjects for study.
    d. measurement.
    e. data collection.

15. Which of the following *best* reflects the nomothetic model of explanation?
    a. Professor Guys wishes to explain alienation with causal variables.
    b. Professor Owings wishes to identify all or almost all the reasons why people retire early.
    c. Professor Rumpley wishes to perform an exploratory study of doctor-nurse interactions.
    d. Professor Wong wishes to identify the major causes of religiosity.
    e. Professor Hmong wishes to extend the generalizability of his grounded theory analysis of death anxiety.

16. Which one of the following hypotheses *best* fits the three criteria of causality?
    a. An increase in status attainment causes an increase in age.
    b. An increase in educational attainment causes an increase in status attainment in occupation, controlling for several variables.
    c. An increase in drowning causes an increase in ice cream consumption.
    d. An increase in conservatism causes a religious conversion, controlling for several variables.
    e. More males than females frequent bars.

## DISCUSSION QUESTIONS

1.  Discuss the reasons why a social scientist would do an exploratory study, a descriptive study, and an explanatory study. Select a research topic and show how this topic would be addressed in terms of each of the three purposes of research.

2.  Professor Nelson is doing a study on the effects of the following variables on the drinking behavior of college students: class level, gender, number of high school extracurricular activities the student participated in, drug usage in high school, family stability during early adolescence, and religiosity. She has a grant to study 800 college students at one point in time and wishes to make some causal assertions. Discuss how she can approximate a longitudinal study, and discuss the types of causal assertions she can legitimately make. Also discuss the limitations on these assertions. Be specific, and use some or all of the variables in your answer.

3.  Explain why causes that are both necessary and sufficient are difficult to identify in the social sciences.

4.  A fellow student who has not taken research methods comes to you for assistance in developing a research project. Which of the research design issues discussed in this chapter would you suggest he address? Why? In what order? Why? What would be your response to his question: "Which of these is the most important?" Why did you respond as you did?

## EXERCISE 4.1                    Name_____

Make up examples for the following units of analysis. Do not use examples from the text, the review questions, or this paragraph. Students often confuse groups and organizations. Think of groups as smaller units than organizations, although in both instances you are studying the collectivity instead of the individuals within the collectivity. Hence a family would be a group and a corporation would be an organization. Also, groups have a specific group boundary; families are groups but women or blacks are categories of individuals. Finally, people typically generally know all or most of the other members in a group but not in an organization. So, a local sorority would be a group but the national sorority would be an organization. The adult Sunday School class would be a group but the larger church would be an organization.

1. Give three examples of topics that involve studying individuals as the unit of analysis.

2. Give three examples of topics that involve studying groups as the unit of analysis.

3. Give three examples of topics that involve studying organizations as the unit of analysis.

4. Give three examples of topics that involve studying artifacts as the unit of analysis.

## EXERCISE 4.2                                Name_____

Select a topic of interest. Select just one variable.  This variable should be something that can vary over time and that is related to the variable age. Examples might include: voting in an election or level of prejudice. Think of other examples. Then show how that variable could be studied in each of the four research designs: cross-sectional, trend, cohort, and panel. Explain the designs for your variable.

Your variable:

Cross-sectional study:

Trend study:

Cohort study:

Panel study:

# EXERCISE 4.3                                 Name_____

A key focus of this chapter is causality—identifying factors (independent variables) that affect other factors (dependent variables). Your assignment is to practice identifying these variables. Be sure to select sociological variables. Avoid examples used in this workbook or in the textbook, or those used by your instructor.

For example, my causal hypothesis might be, "the higher the incidence of poverty in a community, the higher the crime rate." I'm assuming that poverty is a cause of crime. In order to answer question 5, I'm going to have to show and describe how the three criteria for causation can be applied to my example. The alternative arguments or factors that should be examined before accepting your causal hypothesis refer to the third requirement for a causal relationship—the correlation cannot be explained away by some third variable. For example, perhaps I should examine education; low education can cause poverty, and also low education may prevent people from getting jobs and that may cause them to turn to crime. Hence, there may be no real relationship between poverty and crime once education is controlled. Or perhaps I should examine the proportion of minorities in a community. If discrimination against minorities exists, then the more minority people, the greater the poverty. Also, police may be more likely to arrest minorities. These variables may account for the relationship between poverty and crime in my hypothesis.

1.  Identify a dependent variable—some event, behavior, or attitude that varies from time to time and whose variation you wish to explain. Make sure it is a sociological variable.

2.  Identify an independent variable whose variation you believe might explain variation in the dependent variable you described above. Make sure it is a sociological variable.

3.  State a causal hypothesis for your independent and dependent variables.

(continued)

4.  Explain why you expect the relationship noted in # 3.

5.  Describe the three criteria that need to be met before you can reasonably argue that there is a causal relationship between your two variables. In your discussion, note at least one alternative argument or factor that should be examined before accepting your causal hypothesis (this reflects the third criterion). Apply this alternative factor to your specific hypothesis. Remember that an alternative variable must be related to both your independent and dependent variables such that it explains away the relationship between the independent and dependent variables, in the same way that the size of a fire explains away the relationship between the number of fire trucks on the scene and the amount of damage that occurs. Show how your alternative variable is related to both your independent and dependent variables.

## EXERCISE 4.4

Name *Adam Winchester*

Find a research article of interest in one of the social science journals or select one from the reader you are using in this or another social science course. Alternatively, review one or more of the many newspapers on the Web (www.newspaperlinks.com). Your instructor will tell you which of these two options to use, and may give you an article or list of articles from which to select. Make a copy or bookmark your entry on your browser because this article may be used in later exercises; attach the copy to this exercise if requested to do so by your instructor.

1.  Identify the unit(s) of analysis and explain your answer.

    *The*

2.  Identify the independent and dependent variables and explain your answer.

3.  Identify which of the following designs were employed and explain your answer: cross-sectional, trend, cohort, or panel.

# EXERCISE 4.5                          Name_____

The General Social Survey contained in Appendix 1 contains data for 1978, 1983, 1988, 1993, and 1998. Hence, it allows you to perform a longitudinal analysis. Use SPSS or MicroCase (or another data analysis program as indicated by your instructor) to examine how attitudes toward abortion have changed over those time periods. Run a crosstabulation of ABANY (approve abortion for any reason) by YEAR. Be sure to put YEAR on top (columns) and ABANY on the side (rows), and request column percentages.

1. Present your table below.

2. Summarize the percentage differences across the years.

3. Develop an explanation for the changes.

# EXERCISE 4.6                                    Name_____

Babbie discusses the three criteria for establishing nomothetic causality. Your assignment is to apply these criteria to a crosstabulation of support for capital punishment by gender. Use SPSS or MicroCase (or another data analysis program as indicated by your instructor) to run a crosstabulation of support for capital punishment (CAPPUN) by gender (SEX) (see Appendix 1). Be sure to put SEX on top (columns) and CAPPUN on the side (rows), and request column percentages.

1.  Present your table below.

2.  Summarize the relationship as reflected in the percentage differences.

3.  Apply the three criteria for establishing causality to the relationship between support for capital punishment and gender.

# Chapter 5

## Conceptualization, Operationalization, and Measurement

### OBJECTIVES

1. Restate the argument that anything that is real can be measured.

2. Define measurement and differentiate it from observation.

3. Link the terms conception, conceptualization, and concepts.

4. Differentiate among the following terms: direct observables, indirect observables, constructs, and concepts.

5. Illustrate reification and explain why it is an error.

6. Show how indicators and dimensions contribute to the conceptualization process.

7. Outline the logic behind the interchangeability of indicators.

8. Describe and compare real definitions, nominal definitions, and operational definitions.

9. Select three concepts and develop both nominal and operational definitions for each.

10.  Show how the clarification of concepts is a key element in qualitative research.

11.  Explain why definitions are more problematic for descriptive research than for explanatory research.

12.  Explain why researchers must be clear about the range of variation in a concept that interests them.

13.  Give examples of how the variation between extreme attributes of a variable can affect the operationalization of a concept.

14.  Explain why attributes of a variable should be exhaustive and mutually exclusive, and give examples of each.

15.  Differentiate the following four levels of measurement and give an example of each: nominal, ordinal, interval, and ratio.

16.  Explain why it is important to know the level of measurement for the variables in a study.

17.  Explain when single or multiple indicators should be used to reflect a concept.

18.  Differentiate precision from accuracy by definition and example.

19.  Define reliability and compare these strategies for improving the reliability of measures: test-retest method, split-half method, using established measures, and reliability of research workers.

20.  Define validity and compare these types of validity: face validity, criterion-related validity, construct validity, and content validity.

21.  Describe the tension between reliability and validity.


## SUMMARY

Social scientists believe that anything that is real can be measured. This is accomplished through the twin processes of conceptualization and operationalization. Conceptualization involves specifying what is meant by a concept, while operationalization yields the specific measures. Social scientists also commonly distinguish measurement from observation. Observation is a more casual and passive activity while measurement involves careful and deliberate observations for purposes of describing objects and events in terms of the attributes of a variable. Most of the variables social scientists study do not actually exist in the same way that the book you are reading exists. Instead, they are made up and seldom have a single, unambiguous meaning.

Conception reflects the mental images we have of something. Coming to an agreement about what terms mean reflects conceptualization and results in a concept. Scientists measure three things. First, they measure direct observables–things we can observe simply and directly. Second, they measure indirect observables–less direct methods used to provide inferences about concepts. Third, they measure constructs–theoretical creations based on observations but that cannot be observed directly or indirectly. In short, concepts are constructs derived by mutual agreement from conceptions. We sometimes err by believing that the terms for constructs have intrinsic meaning, an error known as reification.

Conceptualization is the process through which we specify what we mean when we use particular terms. Concepts themselves are not real or measurable; the indicators of a concept provide this function. Indicators are signs of the presence or absence of whatever concept we are studying. Seldom can a single indicator capture the full richness of meaning in most concepts. As a result, social scientists develop multiple indicators arranged around specifiable aspects of a concept, known as dimensions. Multiple dimensions and multiple indicators contribute to a more sophisticated understanding of our concepts.

To the extent that multiple, interchangeable indicators produce similar findings, researchers can reach similar conclusions about general concepts, even if they disagree about definitions. This stance is based on the assumption that if different indicators all represent the same concept, then all of them will behave the same way that the concept would behave if it were real and observable.

Three types of definitions contribute to conceptual order. Real definitions reflect the essential nature of a concept but are not very useful in the measurement process. Conceptualization instead depends on nominal and operational definitions. A nominal definition is one that is assigned to a term in a given study, and an operational definition details the specific operations involved in measuring the concept. These elements of conceptualization underscore the process nature of this step and produce conceptual order so that communication and measurement can proceed. Interestingly, definitions are more problematic for descriptive research than for explanatory research because the goal of descriptive research is to describe something accurately.

Social scientists have a variety of options available regarding the measurement process. For one, they must decide on the range of variation appropriate for a given concept. This choice is influenced by the nature of the study and the expected distribution of attributes among the subjects under study. Another choice pertains to how fine the distinctions will be among the various possible attributes of a given variable. This choice is also influenced by the purpose of the study, and social scientists generally err on the side of gathering too much detail rather than too little when they are unsure about how to proceed.

Many times the selection of specific indicators for a variable is quite straightforward because such variables have obvious single indicators (such as age). Other variables are better operationalized through composite measures that combine a number of indicators reflecting separate dimensions (such as religiosity). In either case, attributes for a variable need to be both exhaustive (a complete list of attributes) and mutually exclusive (no overlapping attributes).

Different variables may represent different levels of measurement. Nominal measures employ numbers for classification purposes only; their attributes have only the characteristics of exhaustiveness and mutual exclusiveness. Variables whose attributes may be logically rank-ordered are ordinal measures; the numbers employed reflect relatively more or less of the variable being measured. The actual distance separating attributes in interval measures can be described as being equal, but interval measures have no absolute zero. Ratio measures do have an absolute zero value, enabling the calculation of ratios. It is important to identify the levels of measurement of the variables because analytical techniques vary according to the level of measurement of a variable.

Social scientists apply several criteria to enhance measurement quality. They strive to develop measures that are both precise and accurate. They pay particular attention to reliability (consistency) and validity (actually measuring the concept of interest). Problems with both appear repeatedly in social research. Reliability can be enhanced by asking people only things they are likely to know, by asking the same information more than once (test-retest method), by randomly assigning items to two sets and comparing the responses in the two sets (split-half method), and by using measures known for their reliability. Consistent application of the research design is also mandatory, what is known as research worker reliability.

Validity can be enhanced through establishing face validity, whereby measures are compared with common agreements about a concept and with a logical understanding of a concept. Criterion-related validity (or predictive validity) is based on an external criterion. Construct validity is based on the way a measure relates to other variables within a system of theoretical relationships. Finally, content validity refers to the extent to which a measure covers the range of meanings included in a concept. Social researchers need to consider both their colleagues and their subjects as sources of agreement on the measurement of concepts. Researchers also need to be sensitive to the trade-offs between validity and reliability in their quest for sound measurements.

## TERMS

1. accuracy
2. concept
3. conception
4. conceptualization
5. constructs
6. construct validity
7. content validity
8. criterion-related validity
9. dimension
10. direct observables
11. exhaustive
12. face validity
13. indicators
14. indirect observables
15. interchangeabilty of indicators

16. interval measure
17. measurement
18. mutually exclusive
19. nominal definition
20. nominal measure
21. operational definition
22. ordinal measure
23. precision
24. ratio measure
25. real definition
26. reification
27. reliability
28. split-half method
29. test-retest method
30. validity

## MATCHING

_____ 1. Careful, deliberate observations of the real world in order to describe objects and events in terms of the attributes composing a variable.

_____ 2. The process through which we specify what we will mean when we use particular terms.

___   3.   Real, observable things that give evidence of the presence or absence of the concept we are studying.

___   4.   The definition that is *assigned* a term.

___   5.   The definition that specifies the operations involved in measuring a concept.

___   6.   Reflects the consistency or repeatability of a measure.

___   7.   Reflects the extent to which a measure accurately reflects the concept we wish to measure.

___   8.   A method for establishing reliability that involves splitting a set of items into two halves and seeing how strongly the two correlate.

## REVIEW QUESTIONS

1.   Which one of the following is *false*? Or are they all true?
     a. The concept ethnicity represents the term ethnicity.
     b. Ethnicity is both a concept and a variable.
     c. Ethnicity as a variable is composed of attributes.
     d. Ethnicity may have different definitions.
     e. All are true.

2.   The number of times one swims a week as used to measure physical fitness is an example of a/an
     a. operational definition.
     b. indicator.
     c. concept.
     d. dimension.
     e. construct.

3.   Which of the following is *least* likely to be a dimension of marital happiness?
     a. shared financial decision making
     b. sexual compatibility
     c. similar child rearing ideas
     d. couple communication

   e. length of courtship

4. Professor Lewis spends a few weeks working through what she means by feminism. She decides that it includes such areas as equal treatment before the law,
   equality in the job market, and belief in the equality of men and women. She then
   develops specific questions for each of these three areas, such that the sum of the
   items creates a feminism score. In this example, which of the following reflects
   conceptualization?
   a. the whole process
   b. the term *feminism*
   c. the three basic areas
   d. the calculation of a feminism score
   e. the questions

5. Which of the following *best* reflects interchangeability of indicators?
   a. Joe uses multiple indicators and then deletes two and adds three on the basis
      of a test for reliability.
   b. Cathy decides to use several indicators of one of her variables to improve
      validity.
   c. Lisa decides to use several indicators of both her variables to improve validity.
   d. James argues that it really doesn't matter which of the indicators of his depend-
      ent variable is used because whatever relationship exists between the depend-
      ent and independent variables will appear with any of the indicators.
   e. Susan argues that indicators can be exchanged across dimensions and that the
      reliability and validity as well as the basic relationship will not be altered.

6. Professor Foxdire has been working with the concept of stress for several years
   and has seriously worked at developing a precise measure of stress. He then
   works harder at discovering the real meaning of stress and finally decides that
   stress is real and his measure genuinely reflects it. What error has he made?
   a. provincialism
   b. interchangeability
   c. objectification
   d. ecological fallacy
   e. reification

7. In operationalizing approval for abortion, Professor Oliver is particularly concerned that the measure will reflect those opposed to abortion as well as those
   with varying levels of approval. Which operationalization choice is he confront-
   ing?

a. range of variation
b. number of dimensions
c. number of indicators
d. variation between the extremes
e. interchangeability of indicators

8. Professor Wilson decides to study academic aspiration and, in line with the general thinking on the concept, specifies that she will treat it as the highest degree desired. This is an example of a/an
   a. categorical definition.
   b. nominal definition.
   c. real definition.
   d. empirical definition.
   e. operational definition.

9. Operational definitions are more problematic for descriptive research than for explanatory research because
   a. interpretations of descriptive statements directly depend on operational definitions used.
   b. interpretations of explanatory statements directly depend on the causal connection between concept and operational definition.
   c. in explanatory research operationalization of concepts is irrelevant as long as causality is established.
   d. descriptive statements demand less specificity than do explanatory statements.
   e. explanatory research deals primarily with relationships between variables and not operational definitions.

10. Read the following item and then answer the question that follows: "What is your student status?"
    1. First-year
    2. Sophomore
    3. Junior
    4. Senior
    5. Transfer

    Which of the following *most* accurately describes this question?
    a. It is exhaustive but not mutually exclusive.
    b. It is mutually exclusive but not exhaustive.
    c. It is both exhaustive and mutually exclusive.
    d. It is neither mutually exclusive nor exhaustive.

    e. It is both reliable and valid.

11. Grade point average reflects which level of measurement?
    a. nominal
    b. ordinal
    c. linear
    d. ratio
    e. interval

12. The importance of levels of measurement lies in
    a. distinguishing qualitative from quantitative research.
    b. clarifying the conceptualization process.
    c. determining which statistical techniques are appropriate.
    d. clarifying the operationalization process.
    e. constructing measures of the same concept at different levels of measurement.

13. Which one of the following is *false*?
    a. Precision is more important in descriptive than in explanatory research.
    b. Precision is less important than validity.
    c. Precision parallels validity.
    d. Operationalization enhances precision.
    e. A measure can be precise without being accurate.

14. Professor Garcia decides to employ 60 interviewers in his study of teacher militancy. Which one of the following most likely will be the *major* measurement concern?
    a. epistemology
    b. validity
    c. reliability
    d. conceptual adequacy
    e. ability to interchange the indicators

15. Personnel Director Putler develops a measure of job satisfaction. She shows it to a couple of other personnel directors to make sure her scale measures what it purports to measure. She is seeking
    a. reliability.
    b. precision.
    c. face validity.
    d. accuracy.
    e. indicator correlation.

16. Professor Peoples develops a new scale to measure love. When given repeatedly, it generally yields similar results. When correlated with a well-validated love scale, it shows a low correlation. Which one of the following statements is correct?
    a. The scale is reliable but not valid.
    b. The scale is valid but not reliable.
    c. The scale is both reliable and valid.
    d. The scale is neither reliable nor valid.
    e. The scale is generalizable but not precise.

17. Marketing Analyst Harris tests the validity of her new customer satisfaction scale by testing its relationship to other variables found to be related to other customer satisfaction scales. She is using which type of validity?
    a. face
    b. criterion-related
    c. content
    d. construct
    e. multidimensional

## DISCUSSION QUESTIONS

1. Present a case that we can measure anything that exists. Use examples.

2. Describe the process of conceptualization and operationalization.

3. Discuss why it is important to consider the levels of measurement of variables in doing research.

4. Differentiate reliability from validity. Which is more important? Why?

## EXERCISE 5.1                                    Name_____

Select one of the following concepts: religiosity, feminism, patient anxiety, or marital happiness. Go through the measurement process by completing the steps below. In the first question, describe the conceptualization process that you would go through in measuring the concept you selected. Explain how (i.e., where you would get your ideas on what to include in your definition) you would develop a nominal definition for it, how you would develop an operational definition of it, and how you would actually measure it. In the second question, be sure your nominal definition of the concept makes sense. Your indicators (in the third question) should be measures of the various characteristics or qualities that you have stated in your nominal definition; that is, your indicators should correspond to your nominal definition.

1.  Describe the conceptualization process you would employ to measure this concept. Be specific. Be sure your response reflects the conceptualization process.

2.  Provide a nominal definition of the concept.

3.  Describe indicators you would use in developing your operational definition.

# EXERCISE 5.4

Name_____

The concept of attitude toward pornography might be measured with the following four items. Respondents could be asked to indicate if they thought that:

   a. sexual materials lead to breakdown of morals
   b. sexual materials lead people to commit rape
   c. sexual materials provide an outlet for bottled-up impulses
   d. sexual materials provide information about sex

1. Speculate about the conceptualization process that produced these items. That is, speculate about the thinking process a social scientist might have gone through to develop these four items to measure attitude toward pornography.

2. Explain how three of the four types of reliability techniques could be applied to the items.

3. Explain how three of the four types of validity techniques could be applied to the items.

**EXERCISE 5.5**                    Name_____

Sue is 20 years old and Mary is 40 years old. Write a simple statement regarding Sue's and Mary's ages that illustrates each of the levels of measurement.

1. Nominal:

2. Ordinal:

3. Interval:

4. Ratio:

# EXERCISE 5.6

Name_____

Use the General Social Survey in Appendix 1 to locate one example for each of the following levels of measurement: nominal, ordinal, interval, and ratio. Use SPSS or MicroCase (or another data analysis program as indicated by your instructor) to run frequencies on each one. Reminder: if the last category in what appears to be an interval or ratio level variable includes an attribute of "X or more" (such as "8 or more"), then it no longer is an interval or ratio level variable because the intervals are not equal.

1.  Report the frequencies for each variable: nominal, ordinal, interval, and ratio.

2.  Summarize the results for each variable: nominal, ordinal, interval, and ratio.

# EXERCISE 5.7                                    Name_____

The split-half method for establishing reliability involves splitting your items into two halves and then seeing how well the scores on those two halves correlate. This exercise involves determining how reliably three items measure anomia, the degree to which people feel about their relations with society.  As a modified split-half approach, use SPSS or MicroCase (or another data analysis program as indicated by your instructor) to see how the three indicators of anomia included in the General Social Survey (see Appendix 1) correlate. That is, run crosstabulations of ANOMIA5 with ANOMIA6, ANOMIA5 with ANOMIA7, and ANOMIA6 with ANOMIA7. Because we are not suggesting that one is an independent variable and the other a dependent variable, you can put whichever ones you wish on the top (columns) and side (rows). But request both column and row percentages to facilitate your analyses.

1.  Report the table for ANOMIA5 with ANOMIA6.

2.  Report the table for ANOMIA5 with ANOMIA7.

3.  Report the table for ANOMIA6 with ANOMIA7.

4.  Analyze the degree to which these three items reliably measure anomia.

# Chapter 6

## Indexes, Scales, and Typologies

## OBJECTIVES

1. Link the contents of this chapter with the previous chapter on conceptualization, operationalization, and measurement.

2. List three reasons why composite measures are frequently used in social science research.

3. Differentiate index from scale by definition and example.

4. List the two reasons why scales are generally superior to indexes.

5. Describe two misconceptions regarding scaling.

6. List the four steps involved in creating an index.

7. Define and illustrate face validity, unidimensionality, and variance as criteria for selecting items.

8. Describe the rationale and application for employing bivariate relationships among items in index construction.

9. Describe the rationale and application of employing multivariate relationships among items in index construction.

10. Describe how items can be scored in index construction.

11. Describe five strategies for handling missing data in index construction.

12. Compare the rationale and application of item analysis and external validation as strategies for validating an index.

13. Describe the logic and procedures of the Bogardus social distance scale.

14. Describe the logic and procedures of Thurstone scales.

15. Describe the logic and procedures of Likert scaling.

16. Describe the logic and procedures of the semantic differential.

17. Describe the logic and procedures of Guttman scaling.

18. Explain the coefficient of reproducibility.

19. Explain and illustrate how typologies are used in social science research.

## SUMMARY

Composite measures of variables—indexes, scales, and typologies—are created by combining two or more separate empirical indicators into a single measure. Social scientists employ composite measures for several reasons: single indicators are seldom sufficient to measure a complex concept adequately; multiple items extend the range of scores available; and composite measures are efficient strategies for handling multiple items.

Both scales and indexes are typically ordinal composite measures of concepts. Indexes are constructed by accumulating scores assigned to individual attributes, and scales are constructed through the assignment of scores to patterns of attributes. Hence a scale takes advantage of any intensity structure that may exist among the attributes and conveys more information than does an index.

The first step in constructing an index is selecting items. The items must have face validity (logical validity) and be unidimensional (represent only one dimension). Each item should contain some variance, although the amount may be greater for some items than for others. The next step is to examine the relationship among the items to determine if the items are related to each other empirically; this can be done with percentage tables or correlation coefficients. Bivariate analysis of the items is used to identify those items that should be eliminated either because they are unrelated to the other items or because they are so closely related as to be redundant. Multivariate analysis of the items allows the researcher to determine whether each item adds something to the index independently of the other items.

Next comes scoring the items in an index. The researcher must decide on the desirable range of index scores and must attain both a range of measurement in the index as a whole and an adequate number of cases at each point in the index. The researcher must also decide whether to weight the items equally or differentially; equal weighting is typically employed. The scoring process must include provisions for handling missing data. Several strategies are available for doing so, such as excluding those cases with missing data from the construction of the index, treating missing data as one of the available responses, assigning the middle value, or using proportions based on what is observed.

The last step in index construction is to test for validity. In item analysis, the researcher examines the extent to which the composite index is related to the individual items. External validation is employed by testing the index against other indicators of the same concept. External validation sometimes presents a dilemma. If the index is found to be unrelated to the external validator, it may be hard to decide which is invalid—the index or the other indicator.

The Bogardus social distance scale is used to measure people's willingness to associate with members of different groups. The scale contains an intensity structure by reflecting varying degrees of closeness tolerated. Hence, one can predict which items were selected on the basis of a single score.

When a logical structure among the indicators is not clear, Thurstone scaling may be employed to develop a format for organizing items that have at least an empirical structure among them. Experts are asked to assign numerical scores to many indicators of the same variable; this score reflects how strongly the item reflects the concept. Items on which there is little agreement are eliminated as ambiguous, and several of the remaining items are selected to represent each scale score from the lowest value to the highest value. Scores are generally assigned on the basis of the items selected that have the highest value. Thurstone scaling is infrequently used today because of the time required to construct the scale.

Likert scaling was originally designed to determine the relative intensity of different items. Likert scaling is seldom used today. However, the item format devised by Likert is very popular. Typically, it is used to create simple indexes which consist of a series of questionnaire items with a uniformly scored set of ordinal response categories expressing varying degrees of agreement. Composite scores are calculated by adding the individual item scores. Like the Likert format, the semantic differential asks respondents to choose between two polar opposite positions. Researchers using this procedure must determine the appropriate dimensions for a concept and then find two opposite terms to represent the polar extremes along each dimension.

Guttman scaling is also based on the fact that some items may prove to be "harder" indicators of a concept than others. An important objective of Guttman scaling is to maximize the reproducibility of response patterns from a single scale score. The coefficient of reproducibility reflects the percentage of original responses that could be reproduced by knowing the scale scores used to summarize them. Coefficients above .90 are necessary to conclude that a scale exists.

Whereas indexes and scales provide measures of a single dimension, typologies are often employed to examine the intersection of two or more dimensions. Typologies are very useful analytical tools and can be easily used as independent variables, although the fact that they are not unidimensional makes it difficult to analyze them as dependent variables.

## TERMS

1.  Bogardus social distance scale
2.  coefficient of reproducibility
3.  composite measure
4.  data reduction devices
5.  external validity
6.  face validity
7.  Guttman scaling
8.  index
9.  index validity
10. intensity structure
11. item analysis
12. Likert scale
13. mixed types
14. scale
15. scale types
16. semantic differential
17. Thurstone scaling
18. typology
19. unidimensionality
20. variance

## MATCHING

___ 1. The general class of ordinal measures constructed through the simple accumulation of scores assigned to individual attributes.

___ 2. The general class of measures constructed through the assignment of scores to patterns of attributes; hence it contains an intensity structure.

___ 3. The criterion for choosing indicators that emphasizes the importance of selecting items that logically reflect the concept being measured.

___ 4. The element of a composite measure that indicates that the measure reflects only one dimension.

___ 5. A measure of internal validity that involves examining the extent to which the composite measure is related to (or predicts responses to) the items in the index itself.

___ 6. The generalizability of the results of a measure.

___ 7. A type of index in which response categories reflect intensity of agreement and that assumes that each item has the same intensity as the others.

___ 8. A measure summarizing the intersection of two or more variables.

## REVIEW QUESTIONS

1. The *major* reason for using composite measures is that
   a. they enhance reliability.
   b. they enhance external validity.
   c. they yield validity coefficients.
   d. they yield more comprehensive measures with a wider range of scores.
   e. they enhance the conceptualization process, thereby strengthening the theory.

2. Which of the following is *not* a composite measure? Or are they all composite measures?
   a. scales
   b. indicators

    c. indexes

    d. typologies

    e. all are composite measures

3. The key difference between scales and indexes is that scales
   a. are generally longer.
   b. require more conceptualization.
   c. take into account the different strengths of the indicators.
   d. are more valid and reliable.
   e. assist in building typologies.

4. Professor Leet has developed several items to measure self-concept and checks with a few experts to make sure that his items logically represent self-concept. Which criterion of item selection is he using?
   a. unidimensionality
   b. face validity
   c. internal strength
   d. reproducibility
   e. variance

5. In performing bivariate analyses of items, which is the *most* desirable outcome?
   a. Some relationships should be low, but most should be moderate.
   b. None should be negligibly correlated, but most should be moderately correlated.
   c. All should be very strongly related.
   d. All but a few should be very strongly correlated.
   e. All should be strongly correlated.

6. Which of the following should occur after examining the bivariate relationships among items but before combining items into an index?
   a. calculating a coefficient of reproducibility
   b. validating the index
   c. examining multivariate relationships among items
   d. assessing the reliability of the items
   e. examining response patterns across the answer categories per item

7. The two basic decisions to be made in index scoring are
   a. range of scores and weighting of items.
   b. weighting of items and number of items.
   c. number of items and scalability.

    d. scalability and validity.
    e. validity and range of scores.

8. Professor Bigelow examines the extent to which each item in her fatalism index correlates with the index. Which strategy for index validation is she using?
    a. split-half
    b. parallel forms
    c. item analysis
    d. external validation
    e. face validation

9. Professor Strike wishes to develop a composite measure of adjustment to retirement such that an ordinal scale can be calculated based on items with the same or similar ranges of intensity. Which of the following would be *best*?
    a. semantic differential
    b. Guttman scale
    c. Bogardus social distance scale
    d. Thurstone scale
    e. Likert scale

10. Professor Howitzer wishes to develop a composite measure of teaching effectiveness by using several dimensions, each with several possible answers between two extremes. The polar extremes are to be labeled. Which of the following would be *best*?
    a. semantic differential
    b. Guttman scale
    c. Bogardus social distance scale
    d. Thurstone scale
    e. Likert scale

11. Professor Delaney wishes to construct a composite measure of job satisfaction but is particularly concerned that the items selected reflect equal intervals. He does this by having experts rate each of the items and then he selects 11 items to represent the range of scores. Which of the following did he use?
    a. semantic differential
    b. Guttman scale
    c. Bogardus social distance scale
    d. Thurstone scale
    e. Likert scale

12.  Professor Feyen wishes to develop a composite measure of abortion support such that she can accurately predict which items a respondent agrees with based on the score. Which of the following would be *best*?
     a.  semantic differential
     b.  Guttman scale
     c.  Bogardus social distance scale
     d.  Thurstone scale
     e.  Likert scale

13.  The key difference between typologies and composite measures is that typologies
     a.  are more valid.
     b.  are more reliable.
     c.  reflect interval and ratio levels of measurement and hence allow more powerful statistics.
     d.  contribute more to conceptual clarification.
     e.  are built with more than one variable.

14.  One particular weakness of typologies is that
     a.  they have little validity.
     b.  they have little reliability.
     c.  it is difficult to use them as dependent variables.
     d.  it is difficult to use them as independent variables.
     e.  they are difficult to analyze empirically.

## DISCUSSION QUESTIONS

1.  Give three reasons for the frequent use of indexes and scales in social science research.

2.  What do indexes and scales have in common? How are they different?

3.  Describe the four steps in constructing an index: (1) selecting possible items, (2) examining their empirical relationships, (3) combining some items into an index, and (4) validating the index. Provide specific advice for completing each step.

4.  Compare and contrast the following scaling procedures: Likert, Thurstone, and Guttman. For each, note purpose, advantages, disadvantages, and procedures.

5.  Describe the utility of typologies.

# EXERCISE 6.1                              Name_____

You are to develop a semantic differential scale for a concept of interest. Be sure to follow the advice presented in the chapter.

1.  Identify your concept.


2.  List at least five dimensions that adequately reflect your concept. Remember, dimensions are different aspects of a variable. For example, religiosity has a belief dimension, a ritual dimension, an experiential dimension, and so forth.


3.  Set up the items to resemble Figure 6-5 in the text, and include both the polar opposite terms and the ratings in between.


4.  Describe how you would score the results.

# EXERCISE 6.2                          Name_____

Develop a typology in an area of interest. Explain why you selected the two or more dimensions in your typology. Present your typology in a format like that in Table 6-4 in the text. Explain the typology and show how it could be used in a research study. Be specific.

As you construct your typology, be sure that each of the cells makes sense. For each cell in the table, be sure you can imagine some person (or whatever your unit of analysis) who could have the combination of qualities described for that cell.

1.  Identify your area of interest.


2.  Identify the two or more dimensions in your typology and explain why you selected them.


3.  Present your typology in a format like that in Table 6-4 in the text.


4.  Explain your typology and show how it could be used in a research study.

## EXERCISE 6.3                               Name_____

Select an article from the *Electronic Journal of Sociology* (www.sociology.org), the *Journal of Criminal Justice and Popular Culture* , *Culture* (www.albany.edu/scj/jcjpc), or another online journal article as advised by your instructor. Or find a published sociological research article. Be sure to select an article that includes an index or scale.

1.  Describe the index or scale in your article.

2.  Assess the index or scale in terms of the criteria noted in the text.

**EXERCISE 6.4**                          Name_____

The chapter reviews four basic steps in constructing an index: (1) selecting possible items, (2) examining their empirical relationships, (3) combining some items into an index, and (4) validating the index. You are to apply these steps to the three items in the General Social Survey codebook (see Appendix 1) that measure attitudes toward pornography. The items are PORNINF, PORNRAPE, and PORNOUT. Your instructor will advise you to complete all or only some of these steps.

1.  Regarding item selection, assess these items in terms of face validity, unidimensionality, and variance. To assess variance, you will have to do a frequency distribution on the items. Use the "valid percent" column for your analyses because this column excludes missing values.

2.  Regarding the bivariate relationships among the items, assess these relationships by doing crosstabulations: PORNINF with PORNOUT, PORNRAPE with PORNOUT, and PORNINF with PORNRAPE. Request both column and row percentages. Present the tables below and interpret the results.

(continued)

3.  Regarding the multivariate (in this case trivariate) relationships among the items, use PORNINF as the criterion variable (like Babbie used "basic mechanisms" in Figure 6-4). Your instructor may provide specific instructions on this step.

    For the sake of simplicity, the results should be presented in the following form, although other forms would also be appropriate. Remember that column percentages will not necessarily total 100% since the numbers in your table will only represent those who say "yes" to the PORNINF item.

    "Yes" response on PORNINF

    |              |      | PORNRAPE |      |
    |--------------|------|----------|------|
    |              |      | Yes      | No   |
    |              | Yes  | ___%     | ___% |
    | PORNOUT      |      |          |      |
    |              | No   | ___%     | ___% |

    Interpret the results:

(continued)

4. Regarding index scoring, apply the discussion in the text to this example by creating a new variable, PORN, by summing the three items. Recode the variables first so that "No"=0 and "Yes"=1. Since 1 already reflects "yes," simply recode 2 to 0. The index will reflect the number of items the respondent agreed with. Present a frequency distribution of your index and interpret the results.

5. Regarding index validation via item analysis, validate PORNRAPE by using the index as the independent (column) variable and PORNRAPE as the dependent (row) variable. Do a crosstabulation and request column percentages. Present and analyze the results.

(continued)

6.  Regarding index validation via external validation, validate the index with political views by running a crosstabulation of POLVIEWS by the index you created, PORN. Make POLVIEWS the row variable and PORN the column variable and request column percentages. Present and analyze the results.

# EXERCISE 6.5                              Name_____

Babbie discusses various alternatives for addressing missing values. One of those is to examine other responses of those who have missing values on a variable. Use SPSS or MicroCase (or another data analysis program as indicated by your instructor) to see if there are race and gender differences for those who are missing on the item asking if there are situations that respondents can imagine in which they would approve of a man punching an adult male stranger. That is, run a crosstabulation of HITOK by RACE and SEX. Make HITOK the row variable and RACE and SEX the column variables (run two tables), and request column percentages. The data file may already exclude the two missing values, 8 and 9, from the tables because these values may have already been defined as missing. If this is the case, simply change the coding so that these values are not defined as missing before running your tables. Ignore those with "system missing" values; they were not asked the question. The total number of cases will now be 1,653 instead of the full sample of 2,500.

1.  Report the two tables below.

2.  Analyze the results in terms of who is more likely to have the missing values.

# Chapter 7

## The Logic of Sampling

## OBJECTIVES

1. Define sampling.

2. Document the historical connection between sampling and political polling.

3. Describe and illustrate each of the following types of nonprobability sampling: reliance on available subjects sampling, purposive (judgmental) sampling, snowball sampling, and quota sampling.

4. Describe the role of informants in nonprobability sampling and provide advice on how to select them.

5. Describe the logic of probability sampling, and include heterogeneity and representativeness in your response.

6. List two advantages of probability sampling over nonprobability sampling.

7. Define an EPSEM sample.

8. Define each of the following terms and explain its role in probability sampling: element, population, study population, random selection, sampling unit, and parameter.

9. Using probability sampling theory, describe the sampling distribution.

10. Explain how to interpret a standard error in terms of the normal distribution.

11. Define sampling error and show how confidence levels and confidence intervals are used in interpreting sampling errors.

12. Present an argument that the survey uses of probability theory are not entirely justified technically.

13. Restate Babbie's point regarding making generalizations from sampling frames to populations.

14. Describe simple random sampling and list two reasons why it is seldom used.

15. Summarize the steps in using a table of random numbers.

16. Describe systematic sampling, and employ the concepts of sampling interval, sampling ratio, and periodicity in your description.

17. Link stratified sampling with the principle of heterogeneity and describe how this strategy is executed.

19. Identify the major advantage of multistage cluster sampling and describe how this procedure is executed.

20. Present guidelines for balancing the number of clusters and the cluster size in multistage cluster sampling.

21. Explain why a researcher might use probability proportionate to size sampling, and explain the logic behind this strategy.

22. Outline the rationale for disproportionate sampling and weighting, and note the dangers in using these strategies.


## SUMMARY

Having specified what is to be studied, the next task in the research process is selecting a sample. Sampling affords the social scientist the capability of describing a larger population based on only a selected portion of that population. Two broad types of sampling methods are probability sampling and nonprobability sampling. Some sampling methods are more accurate than others; the early failures and the more recent successes of political pollsters illustrate the refinement of sampling procedures and the increasing reliance on probability methods.

Many research situations preclude the use of probability sampling, especially when it is very difficult or impossible to create lists of the elements to be sample. In these situations, researchers employ nonprobability sampling strategies. Reliance on available subjects is used often, but is a very risky method because it limits the generalizability of the results. Purposive (or judgmental) sampling occurs when a researcher selects a sample based on his or her own knowledge of the population, its elements, or the nature of the research study. Snowball sampling is often used in qualitative field research and is particularly useful when the members of a special population are difficult to locate. It involves collecting data on those members of the target population one is able to find and then asking these respondents to provide information needed to locate other members of that population.

Quota sampling strives to attain representativeness by constructing a matrix representing one or more characteristics of the target population, and then collecting data from persons having the required characteristics of a given cell. But it is often difficult to secure adequate information to create accurate quota frames (the proportions that different cells represent), and bias remains a major problem. As a final nonprobability design, field researchers may sometimes use informants, who are members of the group under study, to provide information about the group itself rather than about themselves. It is best to select informants who adequately represent the group under study, but realize that informants' willingness to respond to outsiders may reflect their marginal status within the group.

Because humans are very heterogeneous, it is important to select samples that adequately represent the population under study. Probability sampling allows the selection of samples not subject to the researcher's biases. A sample is considered representative of the population from which it is selected if the aggregate characteristics of the sample closely approximate those same aggregate characteristics in the population. Hence, probability sampling occurs when every element has an equal chance of being selected (an EPSEM sample). Realize that probability samples rarely represent perfectly the populations from which they are drawn. However, probability samples are more representative than other types of samples, and probability theory permits a statistical estimate of the accuracy or representativeness of a sample.

Probability sampling requires familiarity with several components. An element is that unit *about* which information is collected, and it is typically the unit of analysis of the study. There are two levels to which a sample can be generalized. A population is a theoretically specified aggregation of study elements. A study population is the aggregation of elements from which the sample is actually selected. In random selection, each element has an equal chance of selection independent of any other event in the selection process. Random selection enables us to select elements in such a way that descriptions of those elements portrays accurately the total population. A sampling unit is that element or set of elements considered for selection in some stage of sampling.

Two reasons for using random selection methods are that 1) this procedure serves as a check on conscious or unconscious bias on the part of the researcher, and 2) this procedure is based on probability theory, which yields the basis for estimating population characteristics as well as estimating the accuracy of samples. Probability theory is a branch of mathematics that provides the tools researchers need to devise sampling techniques that yield representative samples and to analyze the results of their sampling statistically. Probability theory provides the basis for estimating the parameters of a population. A parameter is the summary description of a given variable in a population.

The calculation and interpretation of sampling error lies at the root of probability sampling theory and is grounded in the principle of the sampling distribution. The sampling distribution dictates that sample statistics will be normally distributed around the population mean. Probability theory also provides formulas for estimating how closely the sample statistics are clustered around the true population value. This is accomplished through the use of confidence levels (how confident we are that our sample estimate is within a set number of sampling errors of the population value) and confidence intervals (the range between the upper and lower values for a given level of confidence).

However, probability theory operates on a number of assumptions that are seldom met in real-life survey situations, such as: an infinitely large population, an infinite number of samples, and sampling with replacement. Probability theory is useful only to the extent that the researcher can actually select a probability sample. Researchers sometimes overestimate the precision of estimates produced by using probability theory.

A sampling frame is the list of elements from which a probability sample is selected. Difficulties in securing an adequate and accurate sampling frame put constraints on the use of probability theory. Remember that findings based on a sample can be taken as representative only of the aggregation of elements that compose the sampling frame. Researchers sometimes err by extrapolating their findings beyond the population of elements composing the sampling frame.

Simple random sampling is generally assumed in probability applications. This strategy involves assigning a number to each element and using a table of random numbers to select elements for the sample. But simple random sampling is seldom used because it is not generally feasible and it may not be the most accurate method. Systematic sampling is generally preferred over simple random sampling because of simplicity. Once the sampling ratio (the proportion of the population) is determined, the researcher simply selects the elements corresponding to the sampling interval (the distance between elements selected), with the first element selected with a table of random numbers. But researchers must be on guard for periodicity, a cyclical pattern that coincides with the sampling interval.

Stratification may be used with both these strategies, and it increases representativeness by first organizing the sampling frame into homogeneous groups reflecting variables that may be related to the variables under study. Such homogeneous groupings reduce sampling error.

Multistage cluster sampling is most useful when no master list exists to provide a sampling frame. The researcher employs multiple sampling units such that groups of elements are sampled at different stages; the element is the final stage. But this design produces higher sampling errors because each stage yields additional sampling error. A general guideline is to maximize the number of clusters selected while decreasing the number of elements selected per cluster, because clusters tend to be homogeneous. Cluster designs may employ either simple random or systematic sampling, with or without stratification at any of the stages.

When clusters are of varying sizes, it is important to vary the procedure by employing probability proportionate to size sampling. In this modification, larger clusters are given a greater chance of being selected, but the same number of elements are still selected from each cluster. Sometimes a researcher may deliberately or inadvertently overrepresent a segment of the population. When this occurs, weighting can be used to correct for the disproportionate sampling.

# TERMS

1.  available subjects sampling
2.  confidence interval
3.  confidence level
4.  disproportionate sampling
5.  element
6.  EPSEM sample
7.  heterogeneity
8.  informants
9.  multistage cluster sampling
10. nonprobability sampling
11. parameter
12. periodicity
13. population
14. probability proportionate to size sampling
15. probability sampling
16. purposive sampling
17. quota sampling
18. random selection
19. representativeness
20. sampling
21. sampling bias
22. sampling distribution
23. sampling error
24. sampling frame
25. sampling interval
26. sampling ratio
27. sampling unit
28. simple random sampling
29. snowball sampling
30. statistic
31. stratified sampling
32. study population
33. systematic sampling
34. weighting

# MATCHING

___ 1. Another term for probability samples that employ the equal probability of selection method.

___ 2. The theoretically specified aggregation of survey elements to which results obtained from the sample are generalized.

___ 3. A sampling strategy that involves asking members of a special population for information needed to locate others in that population.

___ 4. The summary description of a given variable in a survey sample.

___ 5. The sampling method that employs the EPSEM principle.

___ 6. A probability method of sampling in which every *k*th element in the total list is chosen for the sample.

___  7.  A probability method of sampling in which the researcher ensures that appropriate numbers of elements are drawn from homogeneous subsets of the population.

___  8.  Stopping people at a street corner is an example of this type of nonprobability sampling.

## REVIEW QUESTIONS

1.  The purpose of sampling is to
    a.  enhance reliability of measurements.
    b.  enhance validity of measurements.
    c.  select a set of people with a range of characteristics.
    d.  select a set of people who have the same characteristics as the group from which they are taken.
    e.  extend the quality of conceptualization and measurement.

2.  The failure of several political polls to predict election victories accurately prior to 1950 was due *primarily* to
    a.  samples that were too small.
    b.  failure to use probability designs.
    c.  use of wrong nonprobability designs.
    d.  poor timing.
    e.  faulty questionnaire construction.

3.  Professor Mallory determines the distribution of students on five variables in her target population. She then selects students who fill the pre-established proportions of people in each combination of variables. Which strategy did she use?
    a.  available subjects
    b.  purposive
    c.  stratified
    d.  quota
    e.  weighting

4.  Professor Hilgard wanted to study drug users and began his study by contacting a few drug users that a friend of his knew. He then asked each of these people for the names of other drug users that might be interested in being a part of his study. Which sampling strategy did he use?
    a.  available subjects

    b. snowball
    c. quota
    d. purposive
    e. selecting informants

5.  The *key* feature of probability sampling is that
    a. large samples are taken.
    b. a large proportion of the larger population is selected.
    c. everyone has an equal chance of being selected.
    d. sampling error is eliminated.
    e. people are chosen systematically.

6.  Professor Rosenberg takes a random sample of students from five Michigan public universities and colleges. He then phrases his report in terms of "all Michigan college students." To what group of elements is he generalizing?
    a. parameter
    b. population
    c. study population
    d. sampling unit
    e. sampling frame

7.  Professor Dorfmander did a study on class level and dating at Alexander University. He used the student directory and selected every 15th student. He then mailed questionnaires to them with two follow-ups. He contacted the registrar's office to find out how many students were not listed in the directory. Which one of the following is the sampling frame?
    a. the students on the registrar's list
    b. students both in the directory and not in the directory
    c. the student directory
    d. Alexander University
    e. sampling

8.  Inadequate sampling frames yield problems in establishing
    a. generalizability.
    b. theoretical relevance.
    c. accurate hypotheses.
    d. adequate measurements.
    e. all of the above.

9.  The principle of sampling distribution suggests that

a. one sample is as good as another.
b. many samples of the same population will yield less error.
c. many samples of the same population will yield values evenly spread out across the confidence interval.
d. many samples of the same population will yield statistics that will fall around the population value in a known way.
e. many samples of the same population will yield a lower sampling error than just one sample.

10. Which one of the following distributions of whites and nonwhites in a sample would reflect the most sampling error?
a. 90-10
b. 80-20
c. 70-30
d. 60-40
e. 50-50

11. Professor Gherkey calculated a sampling error of 2 in her study on the proportion of students who voted in the last election. She found that 45 percent voted. What is the 95 percent confidence interval?
a. 41-49
b. 43-47
c. 39-51
d. 44-46
e. 42-48

12. Professor Andrea did a study on the religious behaviors in one Reformed church. She numbered the members and programmed the computer to generate a set of random numbers and print out address labels. Which type of sampling did she use?
a. simple random
b. systematic
c. stratified
d. cluster
e. purposive

13. Professor Connally plans to select a systematic sample of 500 students from a list of 2,000. The sampling ratio would be
a. 4.
b. 10.

c. 8.

d. one-fourth.

e. none of the above.

14. Professor Stampson wishes to take a sample of university students at one university. His main objective is to make sure that the sample is very representative of the larger population in terms of class level and GPA. Which sampling design would be best?

a. simple random

b. systematic

c. stratified

d. cluster

e. snowball

15. Consideration of sampling units is particularly relevant for which type of sampling?

a. cluster

b. systematic

c. stratified

d. proportional

e. simple random

16. Professor Gorenpinsky is interested in doing a study comparing male and female members of the National Organization for Women. Because few men belong, he takes three-fourths of the men but only one-thirtieth of the women, selecting each segment randomly. Which one of the following *best* describes the principle he used?

a. stratification

b. systematic sampling

c. grouping

d. clustering

e. weighting

## DISCUSSION QUESTIONS

1. Suppose you were asked by the principal of a local high school to do a survey of the student body. The principal believes it is sufficient to stop students on their way to the library and hand out the questionnaire. You argue for a probability sample instead. State your argument, and give at least two reasons why probabil-

ity sampling might be preferred. Be sure your analysis incorporates the text discussion on the logic of probability sampling.

2.  Discuss the differences between a population, a study population, and a sampling frame. Use examples. Also discuss the cautions that should be applied in generalizing from the sampling frame to the study population and the population.

3. Explain what a sampling distribution is. Why is it an important concept in making inferences from a sample to a population? Link your analysis to the text discussion on probability sampling theory.

4. Determine which of the nonprobability sampling designs is the most representative and explain why.

## EXERCISES 7.1 and 7.2

The list of sociologists below is taken from a recent version of the *Guide to Members* published by the American Sociological Association and is to be used in Exercises 7.1 and 7.2.

| | |
|---|---|
| 1. Lauren Aaronson | 37. Donald Adamchak |
| 2. Andrew Abbott | 38. Anne Adams |
| 3. James Abbott | 39. Ben Adams |
| 4. Kimberly Abbott | 40. Bert Adams |
| 5. Joan Abbott-Chapman | 41. Darrell Adams |
| 6. Felix Abdala | 42. Douglas James Adams |
| 7. Saleha Abedin | 43. Janet Adams |
| 8. Thomas Abel | 44. Joanne Adams |
| 9. Anthony Abela | 45. Julia Adams |
| 10. Ronald Abeles | 46. Laura Adams |
| 11. Christopher Abells | 47. Michelle Adams |
| 12. Marjorie Abend-Wein | 48. Randolph Adams |
| 13. Joel Aberbach | 49. Rebecca Adams |
| 14. David Aberle | 50. Reed Adams |
| 15. Pnina Abir-Am | 51. Richard Adams |
| 16. Joyce Abma | 52. Stacy Adams |
| 17. Mitchel Abolafia | 53. Christopher Adamson |
| 18. Jill Abood | 54. Michelle Adato |
| 19. Mitchell Aboulafia | 55. Lu Ann Aday |
| 20. Deborah Abowitz | 56. David Aday |
| 21. Gary Abraham | 57. Michele Adcock |
| 22. Brant Abrahamson | 58. Donald Addison |
| 23. Mark Abrahamson | 59. Miriam Adelman |
| 24. Glen Abrams | 60. Richard Adelman |
| 25. Paul Abramson | 61. Pamela Adelmann |
| 26. Jeana Abromeit | 62. Larry Adelmon |
| 27. Lorien Abroms | 63. Evan Adelson |
| 28. James Absher | 64. Francis Adeola |
| 29. Vicki Abt | 65. Maurice Adib |
| 30. Janet Abu-Lughod | 66. Edward Adlaf |
| 31. Rikki Abzug | 67. Chaim Adler |
| 32. Joan Acker | 68. Emily Adler |
| 33. Alan Acock | 69. Gerald Adler |
| 34. Kazumi Adachi | 70. Glen Adler |
| 35. Stephen Adair | 71. Leta Adler |
| 36. Barry Adam | 72. Marina Adler |

## EXERCISE 7.1                                Name_____

Review the box in the text on using a table of random numbers. Using the list of sociologists noted on the previous page and a table of random numbers (see Appendix E in the text), select a simple random sample of ten names.

As you select your sample, you will move through the list of random numbers in the random numbers table. Record below *all* the numbers that you used from the table before you had the numbers necessary for your sample (some will not be used because they are above 72 or are duplicates). Place an asterisk beside the numbers from this original list that you actually used in selecting the names for your sample.

RANDOM NUMBERS USED                SAMPLE OF NAMES SELECTED

____  ____  ____              1. _____

____  ____  ____              2. _____

____  ____  ____              3. _____

____  ____  ____              4. _____

____  ____  ____              5. _____

____  ____  ____              6. _____

____  ____  ____              7. _____

____  ____  ____              8. _____

____  ____  ____              9. _____

____  ____  ____              10. _____

Explain the procedure you followed to obtain the above sample of names.

**EXERCISE 7.2**                    Name_____

Using the list of sociologists, select a stratified systematic sample of approximately ten names, beginning with a random start. The stratification variable, in this case, is gender.

Reorganize the list of names by gender first. This can most easily be done by simply reorganizing the numbers of the names. If a person's gender is not immediately obvious, place the first non-obvious name in the female category, the second in the male category, etc. Then select your systematic sample across the reorganized (i.e., stratified) list.

1. Reorganized list:

2. Please fill in the requested information.

    a. The sampling interval: _____

    b. The random start: _____

    c. The list of names selected:

        1. _____

        2. _____

        3. _____

(continued)

4. _____

5. _____

6. _____

7. _____

8. _____

9. _____

10. _____

11. _____

NOTE:    Correctly drawn systematic samples in this case might result in the selection of 10 or 11 names.

3. Explain the procedure you used in obtaining the above sample.

## EXERCISE 7.3

Name_____

You have received a grant to study drug usage among college students in America. You want to be able to make some generalizations about drug usage among *all* college students in America, generalizations about how many students use drugs, the types and frequency of drugs used, and the characteristics of users (such as age and gender). You will be using a stratified cluster sample in which you stratify on at least two variables and sample at least in two stages. There is no single list that you can get that contains the names of all college students in America. So, what sampling units (clusters) can you select at different stages that will ultimately result in a representative sample of *all* college students? Assume that any college can supply you with a list of all of its students. The variables you stratify on should be relevant to your study and should be those for which you have information. For example, you could stratify on grade level, but not on church attendance since the first, but not the second, would be available on the list of names from a college.

Describe the stratified cluster sample you would use. Stratify on at least two variables and explain why you made the decisions you did in term of which variables to use for stratification. Sample at least two stages, including the final sampling unit. Describe the type of sampling procedure you would use at each stage of sampling and explain why you selected the sampling procedures you did at each stage. Be sure to note how many schools, students, etc. that you have in the various stages of sampling. Discuss the limitations of your sample.

## EXERCISE 7.4                                    Name_____

Select a study published in the journal *Current Research in Social Psychology* (www. uiowa.edu/~grpproc/crisp/crisp.html) or consult your library's online social science journal resources to locate an article. Select an article that includes a description of the sample used. Apply the following sampling issues and concepts to your article. **Warning:** not all social science research articles are appropriate for this assignment since many do not involve and/or fully describe sampling procedures and standard errors. Your instructor may have additional instructions on what to do in such a situation.

1.  Describe briefly the population and study population that the study analyzed.

2.  Describe the sampling frame used in the selection of the sample. Does this differ from the population as described in #1? How?

(continued)

3. Describe the type of sampling design used and explain why it was used. Also discuss any particular advantages and/or disadvantages this design yielded.

4. Briefly interpret and assess the standard errors reported, if any.

5. Determine the extent to which the generalizations made are appropriate for the sampling frame used.

# Part 3

## Modes of Observation

# Chapter 8

## Experiments

## OBJECTIVES

1. Give several examples showing that the experimental mode of observation is particularly appropriate for explanatory purposes.

2. Describe and illustrate with an example the three major pairs of components in the classical experiment.

3. Give an example of the double-blind experiment and indicate why such a design would be used.

4. Contrast the following three strategies for selecting subjects: probability sampling, randomization, and matching.

5. Note the feature that the preexperimental designs have in common, and define and develop examples of each of the following three designs: one-shot case study, one-group pretest-posttest design, and static group comparison.

6. Explain how the following factors may threaten internal validity: history, maturation, testing, instrumentation, statistical regression, selection biases, experimental mortality, and demoralization.

7. Show how the classical experiment handles each of these problems of internal invalidity.

8.  Compare the following true experimental designs: classical design, Solomon four-group design, and posttest-only control group design.

9.  Show how the true experimental designs address the problem of external validity.

10.  Describe how natural experiments occur and give two examples.

11.  Examine the strengths and weaknesses of the experimental method.


## SUMMARY

Experimentation involves taking action and observing the consequences of that action. Experiments are particularly well suited to research topics with limited and clearly defined concepts and hypotheses. The experimental model closely parallels the traditional view of science and is particularly appropriate for explanatory research.

The classical experiment involves three major pairs of elements. Such a design examines the effect of an independent variable (the experimental stimulus) on a dependent variable. Both must be clearly defined. Experimental subjects are randomly assigned to an experimental group and a control group, and both are pretested and posttested on the dependent variable. Control groups are used to control for the effects of the experiment itself. One effect that the experimental stimulus may have is known as the Hawthorne effect, in which attention to subjects may affect posttest scores. Double-blind designs are also used to control the effect of the design. In this design neither the subjects nor the experimenters know which is the experimental group and which is the control group.

The main rule for selecting subjects is to maximize the comparability of the experimental and control groups. This can be achieved through three strategies. Probability sampling involves random selection of subjects from a sampling frame for the two groups; it is seldom used. However recruited, subjects may be randomly assigned to either the experimental group or the control group, a technique known as randomization. Third, subjects in the two groups may be matched on variables thought to influence the dependent variable; this is accomplished through the use of a quota matrix. Randomization is the preferred strategy.

Many social scientific experiments employ what are known as preexperimental designs, so called because they lack a legitimate control group and random assignment. The one-shot case study includes a single group of subjects measured on a dependent variable following the occurrence of some experimental stimulus. The one-group pretest-posttest design adds a pretest for the experimental group but still lacks a control group. The static-group comparison includes a "control group," but neither group is pretested, and subjects are not randomly assigned to each.

Preexperimental designs are particularly prone to internal invalidity. Several factors produce such invalidity. Historical events may occur during the course of the experiment that may confound the experimental results. Maturation may also occur, whereby subjects become more tired, bored, or changed in some other respect. The process of testing and retesting can itself influence people's behavior. Or the measures themselves may not be reliable and valid, a problem known as instrumentation.

Statistical regression becomes a problem when subjects are selected for their extreme scores on the dependent variable. Selection biases enter with many of the methods for selecting subjects. Sometimes subjects drop out of an experiment, known as experimental mortality. Finally, demoralization may set in as feelings of deprivation among the control group result in their giving up.

The classical design involves an experimental group and a control group, both randomly assigned and pretested, and effectively manages the sources of internal invalidity noted above. Two other true experimental designs are the Solomon four-group design and the posttest-only control group design. The former effectively manages the interaction between the testing and the experimental stimulus by adding two additional groups, neither pretested but both posttested and one receiving the experimental stimulus. The posttest-only control group design involves assigning subjects randomly to an experimental and a control group but pretesting neither. These two designs are better than the others in terms of external validity, also known as generalizability.

In their pure form, experiments are usually conducted in a laboratory setting with a high level of researcher control. But not all social phenomena are subject to this kind of control. As a result, researchers sometimes rely on natural experiments to study effects of events that occur in the real world.

The major advantage of experiments is the clear isolation of the experimental variable and its impact on the dependent variable. Experiments are also easily duplicated, which enhances reliability and validity. The greatest weakness of experiments lies in their artificiality. It is not always clear how well the results of laboratory experiments can be generalized to settings outside the laboratory.

## TERMS

| | | | |
|---|---|---|---|
| 1. | control group | 16. | natural experiment |
| 2. | dependent variable | 17. | one-group pretest-posttest design |
| 3. | double-blind experiment | 18. | one-shot case study |
| 4. | experimental group | 19. | placebo |
| 5. | experimental model | 20. | posttesting |
| 6. | experimental mortality | 21. | posttest-only control group design |
| 7. | experimental stimulus | 22. | preexperimental designs |
| 8. | external validity | 23. | pretesting |
| 9. | Hawthorne effect | 24. | quota matrix |
| 10. | history | 25. | randomization |
| 11. | independent variable | 26. | selection biases |
| 12. | instrumentation | 27. | Solomon four-group design |
| 13. | internal invalidity | 28. | static-group comparison |
| 14. | matching | 29. | statistical regression |
| 15. | maturation | 30. | testing |

## MATCHING

____ 1.  In an experiment, the group that receives the experimental stimulus.

____ 2.  The group that does not receive the experimental stimulus.

____ 3.  The method used to ensure comparability of the experimental and control groups; this method assumes that every subject has an equal and known chance of being assigned to either group.

____ 4.  A group of designs that deviate from the principles of the classical design.

____ 5.  A type of experiment in which neither the experimenter nor the subjects know who receives the experimental stimulus.

____ 6.  That which reflects the possibility that the conclusions drawn from the experimental results may not accurately reflect what has gone on in the experiment itself.

___ 7. People continually change and these changes can affect the results of an experiment, which is a source of internal invalidity.

___ 8. A source of internal invalidity in which some events may occur between pretesting and posttesting and which may confound the experimental results.

## REVIEW QUESTIONS

1. Which one of the following is *false* regarding experimentation? Or are they all true?
   a. The experimental model is closely related to the traditional image of science.
   b. Experimentation is especially appropriate for hypothesis testing.
   c. It is better suited for explanatory than descriptive research.
   d. It is especially notable for high researcher control.
   e. All are true.

2. Which one of the following is *not* an aspect of the classical experimental design? Or are they all aspects?
   a. independent and dependent variables
   b. experimental and control groups
   c. high internal validity and high external validity
   d. pretesting and posttesting
   e. all are aspects

3. Professor Stauffer performed an experiment on learning by varying the mode of instruction. She did this for three different grade levels. Which of the following is the experimental stimulus?
   a. mode of instruction
   b. amount learned
   c. anxiety level
   d. grade level
   e. control variable

4. The importance of having a pretest to compare with posttest results lies in
   a. making the sample more random.
   b. comparing the results across pretests.
   c. comparing pretest results with posttest results across groups in the experiment.
   d. making the two groups more equal.

e. comparing the pretest with pretests in other experiments to establish generalizability.

5. An experimenter wanted to see the effects of caffeine intake on the arousal state of her subjects. She randomly assigned subjects to the experimental and control groups and administered caffeine-rich soda to one group of subjects and caffeine-free soda to the other group; she then compared the arousal states of the members of both groups.  This is an example of a
   a. posttest-only control group.
   b. pretest-posttest design.
   c. double-blind experiment.
   d. classical design.
   e. static-group comparison.

6. In the above experiment, caffeine-rich soda and caffeine-free soda, respectively, are the
   a. independent variable and dependent variable.
   b. experimental stimulus and dependent variable.
   c. experimental stimulus and placebo.
   d. placebo and dependent variable.
   e. experimental stimulus and independent variable.

7. Professor Riley performed an experiment in which neither the subjects nor the experimenter knew who got the stimulus. This is an example of which type of experiment?
   a. one-shot case study
   b. classical design
   c. double-blind experiment
   d. static-group comparison
   e. pretest-posttest design

8. Matching refers to
   a. linking subjects in the pretest group with those in the posttest group.
   b. selecting pairs of subjects who are included and not included in an experiment.
   c. selecting similar pairs of subjects and assigning each member randomly to the experimental and control groups.
   d. linking pairs of subjects on the independent variable with those on the dependent variable.
   e. assigning similar pairs of subjects to different settings for the same experiment.

9. Reporter Stocker is involved in testing the effects of watching the news on the emotional health of young children. She decides to use a class of Montessori children and a class of public school elementary children as her experimental and control groups. This is an example of which type of experiment?
   a. double-blind experiment
   b. static-group comparison
   c. classical design
   d. posttest-only control group design
   e. one-shot case study

10. Professor Flannerly performed an experiment on the effects of interpersonal attraction on conflict orientation, but he used different measures of conflict orientation at the pretest and posttest. Which problem of internal validity does this example reflect?
    a. selection bias
    b. testing
    c. experimental mortality
    d. maturation
    e. instrumentation

11. Elmer, a subject in Professor Jencken's experiment testing the effects of certain films on a person's emotional state, has just undergone a break-up with his girlfriend. He continues with the experiment, however. Which one of the following threats to internal validity is reflected in this example?
    a. history
    b. maturation
    c. selection biases
    d. statistical regression
    e. experimental mortality

12. Professor Holsingley conducted an experiment on the effects of lawyer volunteers on parole violations. Those parolees with access to lawyer volunteers had fewer parole violations than those without, but the control group parolees felt left out and committed more crimes as a result. Which problem of invalidity does this example reflect?
    a. regression
    b. statistical regression
    c. instrumentation
    d. demoralization
    e. selection biases

13. External invalidity refers to problems with
    a. randomization into experimental and control groups.
    b. generalizability.
    c. assessing ethical violations.
    d. assessing posttest effects.
    e. selection.

14. What is the basic difference between the classical design and the Solomon four-group design?
    a. There is no difference.
    b. More time elapses between the stimulus and the second observation in the Solomon four-group design.
    c. The Solomon four-group design has randomization.
    d. The Solomon four-group design repeats the classical design but adds groups that are not pretested.
    e. The Solomon four-group design repeats the classical design but adds groups that are not posttested.

15. Natural experiments are most likely to resemble which one of the following designs?
    a. static-group comparison
    b. classical
    c. Solomon four-group
    d. one-group pretest-posttest
    e. posttest-only control group design


## DISCUSSION QUESTIONS

1. Describe the classical experiment. Explain the importance of each of the three major pairs of components.

2.  Compare and contrast the three basic strategies for making the subjects in the experimental and control groups as similar as possible. Which one is best? Why? Which technique is actually used most frequently? Why?

3.  Differentiate internal from external invalidity. Describe at least two factors contributing to each. Which one of the two—internal or external invalidity—is more serious? Why?

4.  Which features of the classical experimental design would be most difficult to incorporate in a natural experiment? Why?

## EXERCISE 8.1                                    Name_____

Your assignment is to design a small-group laboratory experiment that would test the following hypothesis using the pretest-posttest control-group (classical) design:

*Men who work with women who appear clearly more effective than themselves in finding a solution to a problem-solving task will have a higher regard for women than men who work in a group without women on the same task.*

Note: This experiment involves *only* men as subjects. The women are simply confederates and are not part of the basic design. Also, be sure to devise a laboratory experiment.

1. Describe exactly where and how you would select the men for the study. How many men would you select? Why?

2. Describe the experimental and control groups appropriate to the experiment. Describe how you would assign the men to the experimental and control groups.

3. Describe a problem-solving task that might be appropriate for this experiment. That is, develop a problem-solving task that would offer the male subjects the experience of seeing women do better than themselves (the experimental group) or the experience of working on the problem-solving task without the more competent women or without any women (the control group). Again, remember that the women are confederates and are not part of the experimental or control groups.

(continu )

4. Describe the means by which you would test the attitudes of the men in the study regarding their views about women's analytical abilities (in general, not necessarily regarding the women confederates) *prior* to the experiment. This is the *pretest* of attitudes. Provide three sample items.

5. Describe how you would make sure that the confederate women in the experimental group would be clearly more effective in solving the problem than the men.

6. Describe the means by which you would test the attitudes of the men in the study regarding their views about women's analytical abilities (in general, not necessarily regarding the women confederates) *after* the experiment. This is the *posttest* of attitudes. Provide three sample items.

(continued)

7. Describe two potential sources of internal invalidity that your design reduces or avoids. Explain why or how your design does this.

8. Describe one potential source of external invalidity that your design reduces or avoids. Explain why or how your design does this. Remember, external invalidity reflects the generalizability of your results and hence pertains mostly to how you selected your men.

9. Make up some "results" that you might get in such an experiment and interpret them. Be sure to indicate whether the "results" tend to confirm or disconfirm the hypothesis.

## EXERCISE 8.2

Name_____

Your assignment is to conduct an experiment on your friends and acquaintances to examine their sincerity in asking and answering the question, "How are you?" Identify the hypothesis you will test (see the table in #6 first). Your experiment will involve three groups of five subjects each: a control group and two experimental groups. Subjects will be placed in the groups as follows.

*Control Group:* As you meet friends over the next few days, greet five of them by saying, "Hi, how are you?" Record exactly how they answer.

*Experimental Group 1:* For five other friends, allow them to ask how you are first, and reply by saying, "Great, how are you?" Record exactly how they answer.

*Experimental Group 2:* For five other friends, allow them to ask how you are first, and reply by saying, "Terrible, how are you?" Record exactly how they answer.

In assigning friends to the two experimental groups, be sure to alternate "great"and "terrible," saying "great" to one and "terrible" to the next, and so forth. Get people into the control group whenever you are able to beat them to the punch.

1.  Describe your hypothesis:



2.  Responses given by subjects in the control group:

    1. _____

    2. _____

    3. _____

    4. _____

    5. _____

(continued)

3.  Responses given by subjects in Experimental Group 1 ("Great, how are you?"):

    1. _____

    2. _____

    3. _____

    4. _____

    5. _____

4.  Responses given by subjects in Experimental Group 2 ("Terrible, how are you?"):

    1. _____

    2. _____

    3. _____

    4. _____

    5. _____

5.  Score each of the responses as "positive," "neutral," or "negative." For example, a subject who answered "great" would be scored as "positive," one who answered "lousy" would be scored as "negative," and one who answered "so-so" would be scored as "neutral." Your task is to figure out the proper scoring for other kinds of responses. Go back to your answers above and write "positive," "neutral," or "negative" beside each of the responses. *Describe any difficulties you experienced in coding.*

(continued)

6. Complete the table below, entering the percentages of "positive," "neutral," and "negative" responses received from each of the three groups.

|  | Control Group | Experimental Group 1 | Experimental Group 2 |
|---|---|---|---|
| Percent positive | _____ % | _____ % | _____ % |
| Percent neutral | _____ % | _____ % | _____ % |
| Percent negative | _____ % | _____ % | _____ % |
|  | 100% | 100% | 100% |
|  | (5) | (5) | (5) |

7. Provide a brief interpretation of your research findings in light of your hypothesis.

8. Describe the success or failure you experienced in assigning people randomly to the groups.

(continued)

9. Assess this design (not the results themselves) in terms of three sources of internal invalidity.

10. Assess this design (not the results themselves) in terms of external invalidity. (Remember: external invalidity refers to generalizability.)

## EXERCISE 8.3                                        Name_____

You have been asked to develop a study of the effects of watching *Sesame Street* on children's gender-role orientations, intelligence, or sociability (select one). Describe how you would design the study using one preexperimental design: one-shot case study, one-group pretest-posttest design, or static-group comparison—select one. Describe how you would design the study using one true experimental design: prettest-posttest control-group (classical) design, Solomon four-group design, or posttest-only control-group design—select one. Note the major advantage and weakness of each design in this particular study. You might consider the various sources of internal invalidity Babbie mentions as possible weaknesses, although which ones are appropriate varies according to the study design.

1. Dependent variable you selected:

2. Preexperimental design you selected:

3. Describe study using this design:

4. Advantage of preexperimental design:

5. Weakness of preexperimental design:

(continued)

6.   True experimental design you selected:

7.   Describe study using this design:

8.   Advantage of true experimental design:

9.   Weakness of true experimental design:

# EXERCISE 8.4                          Name_____

As a contrived type of natural experiment, we may investigate if owning a gun (the "stimulus") affects propensity toward violence. Use SPSS or MicroCase (or another data analysis program as indicated by your instructor) to test this hypothesis by running a crosstabulation of HITOK by OWNGUN. Make HITOK the row variable and OWNGUN the column variable, and request column percentages.

1.  Report your table below.

2.  Analyze the results to determine if the hypothesis is correct.

# Chapter 9

## Survey Research

## OBJECTIVES

1. Illustrate how surveys may be used for descriptive, explanatory, and exploratory purposes.

2. Describe how surveys are sometimes misused.

3. Differentiate questions from statements by definition and example.

4. Outline the conditions under which open-ended and closed-ended questions are used.

5. List and illustrate several guidelines for asking effective questions.

6. Explain why social desirability is a problem in asking questions.

7. List three guidelines for good questionnaire format.

8. Describe the role of contingency questions and list the principles for their use.

9. Describe the role of matrix questions and list the principles for their use.

10. Explain why the order in which questions are asked is important, and describe how this principle is differentially applied in questionnaires and interviews.

11.  List three principles for providing instructions for respondents of surveys.

12.  List and compare three methods of administering survey questionnaires.

13.  List three methods for distributing self-administered questionnaires.

14.  List three principles for mail distribution and return of questionnaires.

15.  Present an argument for monitoring returns, and show how this can be done with the return rate graph.

16.  List three principles regarding follow-up mailings.

17.  State the response rates that Babbie considers adequate, good, and very good.

18.  Present four advantages of interviews over questionnaires.

19.  Restate the five general rules for successful interviewing.

20.  Discuss the role of specifications in training interviewers.

21.  Describe several elements of interviewer training.

22.  List the advantages and problems with telephone surveys.

23.  Show how computer-assisted telephone interviewing overcomes some of the weaknesses of the telephone survey.

24.  Describe several variations for using computers for administering self-administered questionnaires.

25.  Describe the advantages of online polling and offer some advice for successful online polling.

26.  Contrast self-administered questionnaires, face-to-face interviews, and telephone interviews, and describe when each is most appropriate.

27.  Assess the strengths and weaknesses of survey design.

28.  Give two examples of secondary analysis and/or data archives, and summarize the advantages and disadvantages of this approach.

## SUMMARY

Survey research is the most frequently used mode of gathering data in the social sciences. It consists of selecting a sample of respondents and administering a questionnaire or an interview to them. Surveys may be used for descriptive, explanatory, and exploratory purposes. The unit of analysis is usually the individual, but surveys can be used for other units of analysis as well. Survey research is particularly well suited for studying attitudes and orientations in a large population. Surveys are increasingly used for less legitimate purposes than social research, including marketing surveys and political surveys such as "push polls."

Most concepts are measured through questions and statements. Questions may take one of two forms. Closed-ended questions are easily processed, but sometimes overlook alternative answer categories. Open-ended questions afford a wider range of responses, but they are more difficult to process and may yield irrelevant answers.

Questions should also be relevant to the respondent, very clear, and as short as possible. Respondents should be capable of answering the questions and should be willing to answer the questions. It is best to avoid negative items as well as biased items and terms. Combining two (or more) questions into one is known as a double-barreled question and produces both confusion for the respondent and ambiguity for the researcher. The researcher should also avoid using questions that promote social desirability—answers that make respondents look good. In the final analysis, the overriding guideline is that questions should reflect the purpose of the study.

Questionnaire format and appearance are critical. Questionnaires that are well organized, uncluttered, and attractive reduce the likelihood that respondents will overlook or ignore items or dispose of the questionnaire. The best format for questions is the use of boxes adequately spaced. Contingency questions can help prevent respondents from being confused and annoyed–questions that are relevant to only some of the respondents are identified. A series of questions with the same set of answer categories can be effectively presented through a matrix format, which saves space and time. But occasionally respondents begin marking the same answers without carefully reading the items, a problem known as a response set.

The order of question presentation is also critical because answers to one question can affect answers to later questions. Also, it is usually best to begin questionnaires with the most interesting set of questions to generate interest, although it is generally best to begin interviews with demographic questions to enhance rapport. Clear instructions at the beginning of a questionnaire, as well as at the  beginning of each section, are mandatory. Special situations will require special instructions. Finally, it is important to pretest your  questionnaire to help reduce error. Although it is not essential that pretest participants reflect a representative sample, they should use people for whom the questionnaire is at least relevant.

Self-administered questionnaires are generally executed by mail, although sometimes they are administered to a group of respondents, and sometimes they are delivered and picked up at a later time. Self-mailing questionnaires require no return envelopes, making it easier to return the instrument. Questionnaires can be sent via first-class postage or bulk rate and returned via postage stamps or business-reply permits. When each option would be used is determined largely by the budget and the expected return rate.

Monitoring the returns of questionnaires is an important part of the study and can be accomplished with a return rate graph plotting the number of questionnaires returned each day. Such a graph can provide clues about when follow-up mailings should occur, and it may be useful in estimating nonresponse bias. Follow-up mailings may contain only a letter of additional encouragement or may contain a new copy of the questionnaire as well. Follow-up mailings significantly increase return rates; two follow-ups mailed two or three weeks apart are best.

There are no strict standards for determining an acceptable response rate. High response rates increase the probability that the respondents accurately represent the sample, thus reducing the chance of response bias. But a demonstrated lack of response bias is more crucial than the response rate itself. A response rate of at least 50 percent is adequate, 60 percent is considered good, and 70 percent is considered very good.

Interviews provide a number of advantages over the self-administered questionnaire. They attain higher response rates, decrease the number of "don't know" and "no answer" responses, help correct confusing items, and provide the opportunity to observe the social situation as well as to ask questions.

It is critical that the interviewer serve as a neutral conduit through which questions and answers are transmitted. Interviewers should have a pleasant demeanor and dress in a fashion similar to the people being interviewed. Familiarity with the instrument will lessen the time required and minimize problems with individual items. Interviewers should follow the question wording exactly and record responses exactly.

One particular skill required is probing, whereby the interviewer redirects inappropriate answers while maintaining the neutral role. When multiple interviewers are employed, the researcher should thoroughly train and supervise the interviewers. Researchers should also prepare specifications, which are explanatory and clarifying comments about handling difficult or confusing situations that may arise with a specific item.

Telephone surveys save money and time, sometimes enhance willingness to give socially disapproved answers, and yield greater control when several interviewers are employed. They also alleviate personal safety concerns. But they come with several problems. They have a bad reputation, for example, and people can hang up easily before the interview is completed. Computer-assisted telephone interviewing is frequently used to enhance the reliability and validity of the results. Computer-assisted survey methods are also increasingly being used for in-person interviews as well as for analyzing data as the data are gathered. Recent innovations in computer technology provide several options for computer administered questionnaires. Online polling offers advantages over other forms but comes with some disadvantages, particularly concerning representativeness.

Self-administered questionnaires and interviews each have advantages and disadvantages. Questionnaires are generally cheaper and quicker and are more appropriate in dealing with more sensitive issues. Interviews help reduce incomplete answers, are more effective in dealing with complicated issues, enable a researcher to conduct a survey based only on a sample of addresses, and provide the opportunity to make important observations apart from the responses to the items. Interviews generally yield higher response rates.

The survey design itself has strengths and weaknesses compared to other designs. It is particularly appropriate for describing the characteristics of large populations, thereby making large samples feasible. In some respects, surveys are quite flexible, and the use of standardized questions enhances reliability. But these advantages come at some cost. Standardization often results in overlooking other appropriate responses and may generate inflexibility in modifying questions. Surveys seldom analyze the context of social life. They are frequently labeled as artificial because the topic of study may not be amenable to measurement through questionnaires, and the act of studying that topic may affect the results. In short, survey research is weak on validity and strong on reliability.

Researchers with a need for survey data cannot always afford to conduct large-scale surveys themselves. Hence many researchers employ secondary analysis of data gathered for some other purpose by someone else. Such research has experienced increased popularity due to the establishment of data archives, research centers that collect and distribute many different types of data sets. Such analysis can be done quite rapidly and inexpensively, particularly with those that are online. The key advantages of secondary analysis include the low cost and the ability to use data gathered by well known researchers and data collection agencies. The key problem with secondary analysis is validity; when one researcher collects data for a given purpose, other researchers have no assurance that such data will be appropriate for their research interests. Comparability of measures is a particular problem.

## TERMS

1. bias
2. closed-ended question
3. Computer Assisted Personal Interviewing (CAPI)
4. Computer Assisted Self Interviewing (CASI)
5. Computer Assisted Self-Administered Questionnaire (CSAQ)
6. Computer Assisted Telephone Interviewing (CATI)
7. contingency question
8. data archives
9. double-barreled question
10. interview
11. matrix questions
12. open-ended question
13. probe
14. questionnaire
15. respondent
16. response rate
17. return rate graph
18. secondary analysis
19. social desirability
20. specifications
21. telephone surveys
22. Touchtone Data Entry (TDE)
23. Voice Recognition (VR)

## MATCHING

___  1.  When people answer survey questions through a filter of what will make them look good.

___  2.  The percentage of those sent a survey who return them.

___  3.  Collections of data sets that are available to researchers.

___  4.  A method that helps researchers monitor the flow of questionnaires returned by respondents.

___  5.  A question that asks respondents for a single answer to a question that actually has multiple parts.

___  6.  Explanatory and clarifying comments about the handling of difficult or confusing situations that may occur in an interview situation.

___  7.  A method used by interviewers to obtain elaboration of respondents' answers to open-ended questions.

___  8.  A method of research in which researchers analyze data that another researcher has collected.

## REVIEW QUESTIONS

1.  The *major* problem with closed-ended questions is
    a. the number of items in the questionnaire.
    b. the number of items per dimension.
    c. the order of the answers.
    d. the structuring of the responses.
    e. response set.

2.  Read the following item and then answer the question that follows: "How satisfied are you with your working conditions and wages?"
    1. very satisfied
    2. somewhat satisfied
    3. somewhat dissatisfied

4. very dissatisfied

What is the *major* weakness with this item?
a. It is double-barreled.
b. It is not clear.
c. It is too long.
d. It is not relevant.
e. Respondents may not be competent to answer it.

3.  Read the following item and then answer the question that follows: "How old were you when you first got in a fight with someone other than a sibling?"
    1. two years old or younger
    2. three to five years old
    3. six to seven years old
    4. eight to nine years old
    5. ten years old or older
    6. I have never been in a fight

    What is the *major* weakness with this item?
    a. It is double-barreled.
    b. It is biased.
    c. It is too long.
    d. It is not relevant.
    e. Respondents may not be competent to answer it.

4.  Read the following item and then answer the question that follows: "The main cause of highway accidents is speeding by truckers. Don't you agree that the use of radar detectors by truckers should be made illegal?"
    1. yes
    2. not sure
    3. no

    What is the *major* weakness with this item?
    a. It is socially desirable.
    b. It is too long.
    c. It is biased.
    d. It is double-barreled.
    e. It is not clear.

5.  Read the following item and then answer the question that follows: "How often do you feel that you are basically a kind and loving person?"
    1. all the time
    2. usually
    3. usually not
    4. never

    What is the *major* weakness with this item?
    a. It is socially desirable.
    b. It is too long.
    c. It is not clear.
    d. It is not mutually exclusive.
    e. Respondents may not be competent to answer it.

6.  Which one of the following is the *worst* method for providing space for checking responses? Or are they all equally fine?
    a. boxes
    b. parentheses
    c. brackets
    d. open blanks for check marks
    e. all are equally fine

7.  Professor Kaled wishes to ask three additional questions only of those respondents who have been active in a political organization in the previous year. *Best* to use would be
    a. contingency questions.
    b. matrix questions.
    c. matched questions.
    d. separate questionnaires.
    e. different response sets.

8.  Response set is *most* likely to occur in which kinds of questions?
    a. matrix questions
    b. contingency questions
    c. closed-ended questions
    d. open-ended questions
    e. interview questions

9.  A particularly useful strategy for improving response rates to self-administered questionnaires is to

        a. offer an inducement.
        b. use commemorative stamps.
        c. use colored paper.
        d. use hand delivery and/or pick up.
        e. use a jazzy cover letter.

10.   An important feature of using a return rate graph is to
        a. reduce sampling error.
        b. examine history effects.
        c. examine measurement effects.
        d. estimate nonresponse biases.
        e. improve reliability.

11.   According to Babbie, a 60 percent return rate is considered
        a. poor.
        b. adequate.
        c. good.
        d. very good.
        e. excellent.

12.   Which one of the following is *not* an advantage of interviews over question-
     naires? Or are they all advantages?
        a. increased response rates
        b. safeguard against confusing items
        c. lower numbers of "don't know" and "no answer" responses
        d. increased reliability
        e. all are advantages

13.   Interviewers can be helped in dealing with confusing situations regarding a given
     item through the use of clarifying comments known as
        a. specifications.
        b. elaborations.
        c. matrix questions.
        d. response set formats.
        e. conversations.

14.   Which one of the following is *false* regarding telephone interviews?
        a. They are cheaper than in-person interviews.
        b. They save time over in-person interviews.
        c. They enhance the safety of the interviewer.

d. They make it harder for the respondent to terminate the interview.

e. They have a bad reputation.

15. The major problem with secondary analysis pertains to

    a. theory.

    b. hypotheses.

    c. validity.

    d. sampling.

    e. empirical generalization.

## DISCUSSION QUESTIONS

1. Why is a low response rate of concern in survey research? Why is response bias of concern? Which is a more serious threat to survey results and generalization—low response rates or response biases? Why?

2. Compare and contrast interviews and questionnaires on the several dimensions noted in the chapter.

3.  Write a first draft of a brief guide for new interviewers.

4.  In this chapter Babbie describes many guidelines for asking questions. Discuss how a researcher could best avoid making the errors he describes. Discuss strategies appropriate before, during, and after the question-writing stage.

## EXERCISE 9.1

Name_____

Use the information that follows to construct both types of return rate graphs that Babbie discusses. Then write a short analysis of the results.

A questionnaire was mailed to 1,000 students (both off-campus and on-campus) at Northern Michigan University on March 1. A follow-up was done on March 17. The questionnaires were returned as follows:

| Date | # Received | Date | # Received |
|------|-----------|------|-----------|
| March 6 | 2 | March 26 | no mail |
| March 7 | 5 | March 27 | no mail |
| March 8 | 18 | March 28 | 28 |
| March 9 | 32 | March 29 | 21 |
| March 10 | 35 | March 30 | 23 |
| March 11 | 25 | March 31 | 14 |
| March 12 | no mail | April 1 | 12 |
| March 13 | no mail | April 2 | no mail |
| March 14 | 20 | April 3 | no mail |
| March 15 | 19 | April 4 | 10 |
| March 16 | 20 | April 5 | 11 |
| March 17 | 14 | April 6 | 9 |
| March 18 | 13 | April 7 | 6 |
| March 19 | no mail | April 8 | 5 |
| March 20 | no mail | April 9 | no mail |
| March 21 | 16 | April 10 | no mail |
| March 22 | 26 | April 11 | 2 |
| March 23 | 37 | April 12 | 0 |
| March 24 | 41 | | |
| March 25 | 30 | | |

1. Create a graph that plots the number of questionnaires returned each day.

(continued)

2.  Create a graph that plots the cumulative number over time and percentage of questionnaires returned.

3.  Summarize the results of both graphs.

# EXERCISE 9.2                              Name_____

Each of the questionnaire items below has two or more things wrong with it. Point out at least two defects for each questionnaire item. Rewrite each item to correct the defects. Do not use open-ended questions as a rewrite to fix problems in closed-ended questions.

At the end of the exercise you are asked to identify the appropriate level of measurement for each item.

1. Religion

   Protestant          Jewish
   Catholic            Episcopalian
   Lutheran            Other

Defects:

Rewritten:

2. At what age were you toilet-trained?

   ( )  Before six months old
   ( )  Between six months old and nine months old
   ( )  Between nine months old and one year old
   ( )  Between one year old and one and a half years old
   ( )  Between one and a half years old and two years old
   ( )  Between two years old and three years old
   ( )  Older than three years old
   ( )  Not applicable

(continued)

Defects:


Rewritten:




3.   How much money do you make?  $_____

Defects:


Rewritten:






4.   Suppose you were in a bookstore and saw a book displayed on a counter near the
     door that you wanted very much but could not afford. Would you steal it?

     ( )   Yes                         ( ) No

Defects:


Rewritten:


(continued)

5. Are you a college student or graduate? If so, why did you decide to go to college?

    ( )    I had a thirst for more knowledge
    ( )    I wanted to get a better understanding of the world
    ( )    I was too lazy to get a job

Defects:

Rewritten:

6. Do you agree or disagree that the trouble with welfare is that people get too comfortable and don't want to go back to work, so the government should institute some job-training programs for people on welfare and then set a limited amount of time in which they can learn work skills and get a job?

    ( )   Agree                 ( ) Disagree

Defects:

Rewritten:

7. Do you disagree or agree with the President that the United States shouldn't provide a national health care program?

    ( )   Agree                 ( ) Disagree

(continued)

Defects:


Rewritten:



8.  Where do you get most or all of your information about current events in the nation and the world?

    ( )   Radio          ( )   Newspapers      ( )   Magazines      ( ) Internet

Defects:


Rewritten:



9.  Why do you think big cars are a bad thing for America?

Defects:


Rewritten:

## EXERCISE 9.3                              Name_____

On the following pages are ten copies of a short interview schedule. Your assignment is to select and interview ten people: five men and five women (your instructor may provide additional sampling instructions). Do *not* simply interview your friends. Please be sure to actually interview the respondents; do *not* have them fill out their own questionnaires. Do *not* read out loud the specifications (the comments in all capitals in parentheses).

After completing the interviews, write a short report of your experiences below. Discuss the problems you experienced and how you dealt with them. Which types of probes did you employ? With what success? Which aspects of the advice for interviewing found in the chapter proved to be the most useful? Which proved to be the least useful? What would you do differently now? Why? How? Do not discuss the actual results of the survey.

(continued)

Case ID_____                                Respondent's gender:  [ ] Male  [ ] Female

Hello. My name is _____ and I'm conducting a short survey as part of an exercise for my research methods class. Would you be willing to participate in the study? The interview will take less than five minutes. (ENCOURAGE IF RELUCTANT.)

I'm going to read some opinions about the effects of looking at or reading sexual materials such as X-rated magazines and videos. As I read each one, please tell me if you think sexual materials do or do not have that effect. (READ EACH ITEM AND CHECK THE APPROPRIATE CATEGORY.)

|  | Yes | No | Don't Know | No Answer |
|---|---|---|---|---|
| 1. Sexual materials provide information about sex. | [ ] | [ ] | [ ] | [ ] |
| 2. Sexual materials lead to a breakdown of morals. | [ ] | [ ] | [ ] | [ ] |
| 3. Sexual materials lead people to commit rape. | [ ] | [ ] | [ ] | [ ] |

I am going to name some institutions in this country. As far as the PEOPLE RUNNING these institutions are concerned, would you say that you have a great deal of confidence, only some confidence, or hardly any confidence at all in them? (CODE FOR EACH ITEM; CODE DK FOR "DON'T KNOW" OR NA FOR "NO ANSWER" IF APPROPRIATE.)

|  | Great Deal | Only Some | Hardly Any | DK | NA |
|---|---|---|---|---|---|
| 4. Education | [ ] | [ ] | [ ] | [ ] | [ ] |
| 5. Press | [ ] | [ ] | [ ] | [ ] | [ ] |
| 6. Congress | [ ] | [ ] | [ ] | [ ] | [ ] |

7. Could you tell me, in your own words, how you feel about capital punishment?

That completes the interview. Thank you for your cooperation.

Case ID_____                          Respondent's gender: [ ] Male  [ ] Female

Hello. My name is _____ and I'm conducting a short survey as part of an exercise for my research methods class. Would you be willing to participate in the study? The interview will take less than five minutes. (ENCOURAGE IF RELUCTANT.)

I'm going to read some opinions about the effects of looking at or reading sexual materials such as X-rated magazines and videos. As I read each one, please tell me if you think sexual materials do or do not have that effect. (READ EACH ITEM AND CHECK THE APPROPRIATE CATEGORY.)

|  | Yes | No | Don't Know | No Answer |
|---|---|---|---|---|
| 1.  Sexual materials provide information about sex. | [ ] | [ ] | [ ] | [ ] |
| 2.  Sexual materials lead to a breakdown of morals. | [ ] | [ ] | [ ] | [ ] |
| 3.  Sexual materials lead people to commit rape. | [ ] | [ ] | [ ] | [ ] |

I am going to name some institutions in this country. As far as the PEOPLE RUNNING these institutions are concerned, would you say that you have a great deal of confidence, only some confidence, or hardly any confidence at all in them? (CODE FOR EACH ITEM; CODE DK FOR "DON'T KNOW" OR NA FOR "NO ANSWER" IF APPROPRIATE.)

|  | Great Deal | Only Some | Hardly Any | DK | NA |
|---|---|---|---|---|---|
| 4.  Education | [ ] | [ ] | [ ] | [ ] | [ ] |
| 5.  Press | [ ] | [ ] | [ ] | [ ] | [ ] |
| 6.  Congress | [ ] | [ ] | [ ] | [ ] | [ ] |

7.  Could you tell me, in your own words, how you feel about capital punishment?

That completes the interview. Thank you for your cooperation.

Case ID_____                  Respondent's gender: [ ] Male [ ] Female

Hello. My name is _____ and I'm conducting a short survey as part of an exercise for my research methods class. Would you be willing to participate in the study? The interview will take less than five minutes. (ENCOURAGE IF RELUCTANT.)

I'm going to read some opinions about the effects of looking at or reading sexual materials such as X-rated magazines and videos. As I read each one, please tell me if you think sexual materials do or do not have that effect. (READ EACH ITEM AND CHECK THE APPROPRIATE CATEGORY.)

|  | Yes | No | Don't Know | No Answer |
|---|---|---|---|---|
| 1. Sexual materials provide information about sex. | [ ] | [ ] | [ ] | [ ] |
| 2. Sexual materials lead to a breakdown of morals. | [ ] | [ ] | [ ] | [ ] |
| 3. Sexual materials lead people to commit rape. | [ ] | [ ] | [ ] | [ ] |

I am going to name some institutions in this country. As far as the PEOPLE RUNNING these institutions are concerned, would you say that you have a great deal of confidence, only some confidence, or hardly any confidence at all in them? (CODE FOR EACH ITEM; CODE DK FOR "DON'T KNOW" OR NA FOR "NO ANSWER" IF APPROPRIATE.)

|  | Great Deal | Only Some | Hardly Any | DK | NA |
|---|---|---|---|---|---|
| 4. Education | [ ] | [ ] | [ ] | [ ] | [ ] |
| 5. Press | [ ] | [ ] | [ ] | [ ] | [ ] |
| 6. Congress | [ ] | [ ] | [ ] | [ ] | [ ] |

7. Could you tell me, in your own words, how you feel about capital punishment?

That completes the interview. Thank you for your cooperation.

Case ID_____                          Respondent's gender:  [ ] Male  [ ] Female

Hello. My name is _____ and I'm conducting a short survey as part of an exercise for my research methods class. Would you be willing to participate in the study? The interview will take less than five minutes. (ENCOURAGE IF RELUCTANT.)

I'm going to read some opinions about the effects of looking at or reading sexual materials such as X-rated magazines and videos. As I read each one, please tell me if you think sexual materials do or do not have that effect. (READ EACH ITEM AND CHECK THE APPROPRIATE CATEGORY.)

|  |  | Yes | No | Don't Know | No Answer |
|---|---|---|---|---|---|
| 1. | Sexual materials provide information about sex. | [ ] | [ ] | [ ] | [ ] |
| 2. | Sexual materials lead to a breakdown of morals. | [ ] | [ ] | [ ] | [ ] |
| 3. | Sexual materials lead people to commit rape. | [ ] | [ ] | [ ] | [ ] |

I am going to name some institutions in this country. As far as the PEOPLE RUNNING these institutions are concerned, would you say that you have a great deal of confidence, only some confidence, or hardly any confidence at all in them? (CODE FOR EACH ITEM; CODE DK FOR "DON'T KNOW" OR NA FOR "NO ANSWER" IF APPROPRIATE.)

|  |  | Great Deal | Only Some | Hardly Any | DK | NA |
|---|---|---|---|---|---|---|
| 4. | Education | [ ] | [ ] | [ ] | [ ] | [ ] |
| 5. | Press | [ ] | [ ] | [ ] | [ ] | [ ] |
| 6. | Congress | [ ] | [ ] | [ ] | [ ] | [ ] |

7. Could you tell me, in your own words, how you feel about capital punishment?

That completes the interview. Thank you for your cooperation.

Case ID_____                        Respondent's gender:  [ ] Male  [ ] Female

Hello. My name is _____ and I'm conducting a short survey as part of an exercise for my research methods class. Would you be willing to participate in the study? The interview will take less than five minutes. (ENCOURAGE IF RELUCTANT.)

I'm going to read some opinions about the effects of looking at or reading sexual materials such as X-rated magazines and videos. As I read each one, please tell me if you think sexual materials do or do not have that effect. (READ EACH ITEM AND CHECK THE APPROPRIATE CATEGORY.)

|  |  | Yes | No | Don't Know | No Answer |
|---|---|---|---|---|---|
| 1. | Sexual materials provide information about sex. | [ ] | [ ] | [ ] | [ ] |
| 2. | Sexual materials lead to a breakdown of morals. | [ ] | [ ] | [ ] | [ ] |
| 3. | Sexual materials lead people to commit rape. | [ ] | [ ] | [ ] | [ ] |

I am going to name some institutions in this country. As far as the PEOPLE RUNNING these institutions are concerned, would you say that you have a great deal of confidence, only some confidence, or hardly any confidence at all in them? (CODE FOR EACH ITEM; CODE DK FOR "DON'T KNOW" OR NA FOR "NO ANSWER" IF APPROPRIATE.)

|  |  | Great Deal | Only Some | Hardly Any | DK | NA |
|---|---|---|---|---|---|---|
| 4. | Education | [ ] | [ ] | [ ] | [ ] | [ ] |
| 5. | Press | [ ] | [ ] | [ ] | [ ] | [ ] |
| 6. | Congress | [ ] | [ ] | [ ] | [ ] | [ ] |

7.  Could you tell me, in your own words, how you feel about capital punishment?

That completes the interview. Thank you for your cooperation.

Case ID_____                          Respondent's gender: [ ] Male [ ] Female

Hello. My name is _____ and I'm conducting a short survey as part of an exercise for my research methods class. Would you be willing to participate in the study? The interview will take less than five minutes. (ENCOURAGE IF RELUCTANT.)

I'm going to read some opinions about the effects of looking at or reading sexual materials such as X-rated magazines and videos. As I read each one, please tell me if you think sexual materials do or do not have that effect. (READ EACH ITEM AND CHECK THE APPROPRIATE CATEGORY.)

|  |  | Yes | No | Don't Know | No Answer |
|---|---|---|---|---|---|
| 1. | Sexual materials provide information about sex. | [ ] | [ ] | [ ] | [ ] |
| 2. | Sexual materials lead to a breakdown of morals. | [ ] | [ ] | [ ] | [ ] |
| 3. | Sexual materials lead people to commit rape. | [ ] | [ ] | [ ] | [ ] |

I am going to name some institutions in this country. As far as the PEOPLE RUNNING these institutions are concerned, would you say that you have a great deal of confidence, only some confidence, or hardly any confidence at all in them? (CODE FOR EACH ITEM; CODE DK FOR "DON'T KNOW" OR NA FOR "NO ANSWER" IF APPROPRIATE.)

|  |  | Great Deal | Only Some | Hardly Any | DK | NA |
|---|---|---|---|---|---|---|
| 4. | Education | [ ] | [ ] | [ ] | [ ] | [ ] |
| 5. | Press | [ ] | [ ] | [ ] | [ ] | [ ] |
| 6. | Congress | [ ] | [ ] | [ ] | [ ] | [ ] |

7. Could you tell me, in your own words, how you feel about capital punishment?

That completes the interview. Thank you for your cooperation.

Case ID_____                         Respondent's gender:  [ ] Male  [ ] Female

Hello. My name is _____ and I'm conducting a short survey as part of an exercise for my research methods class. Would you be willing to participate in the study? The interview will take less than five minutes. (ENCOURAGE IF RELUCTANT.)

I'm going to read some opinions about the effects of looking at or reading sexual materials such as X-rated magazines and videos. As I read each one, please tell me if you think sexual materials do or do not have that effect. (READ EACH ITEM AND CHECK THE APPROPRIATE CATEGORY.)

|   |   | Yes | No | Don't Know | No Answer |
|---|---|---|---|---|---|
| 1. | Sexual materials provide information about sex. | [ ] | [ ] | [ ] | [ ] |
| 2. | Sexual materials lead to a breakdown of morals. | [ ] | [ ] | [ ] | [ ] |
| 3. | Sexual materials lead people to commit rape. | [ ] | [ ] | [ ] | [ ] |

I am going to name some institutions in this country. As far as the PEOPLE RUNNING these institutions are concerned, would you say that you have a great deal of confidence, only some confidence, or hardly any confidence at all in them? (CODE FOR EACH ITEM; CODE DK FOR "DON'T KNOW" OR NA FOR "NO ANSWER" IF APPROPRIATE.)

|   |   | Great Deal | Only Some | Hardly Any | DK | NA |
|---|---|---|---|---|---|---|
| 4. | Education | [ ] | [ ] | [ ] | [ ] | [ ] |
| 5. | Press | [ ] | [ ] | [ ] | [ ] | [ ] |
| 6. | Congress | [ ] | [ ] | [ ] | [ ] | [ ] |

7. Could you tell me, in your own words, how you feel about capital punishment?

That completes the interview. Thank you for your cooperation.

Case ID_____                              Respondent's gender:  [ ] Male  [ ] Female

Hello. My name is _____ and I'm conducting a short survey as part of an exercise for my research methods class. Would you be willing to participate in the study? The interview will take less than five minutes. (ENCOURAGE IF RELUCTANT.)

I'm going to read some opinions about the effects of looking at or reading sexual materials such as X-rated magazines and videos. As I read each one, please tell me if you think sexual materials do or do not have that effect. (READ EACH ITEM AND CHECK THE APPROPRIATE CATEGORY.)

|  |  | Yes | No | Don't Know | No Answer |
|---|---|---|---|---|---|
| 1. | Sexual materials provide information about sex. | [ ] | [ ] | [ ] | [ ] |
| 2. | Sexual materials lead to a breakdown of morals. | [ ] | [ ] | [ ] | [ ] |
| 3. | Sexual materials lead people to commit rape. | [ ] | [ ] | [ ] | [ ] |

I am going to name some institutions in this country. As far as the PEOPLE RUNNING these institutions are concerned, would you say that you have a great deal of confidence, only some confidence, or hardly any confidence at all in them? (CODE FOR EACH ITEM; CODE DK FOR "DON'T KNOW" OR NA FOR "NO ANSWER" IF APPROPRIATE.)

|  |  | Great Deal | Only Some | Hardly Any | DK | NA |
|---|---|---|---|---|---|---|
| 4. | Education | [ ] | [ ] | [ ] | [ ] | [ ] |
| 5. | Press | [ ] | [ ] | [ ] | [ ] | [ ] |
| 6. | Congress | [ ] | [ ] | [ ] | [ ] | [ ] |

7.  Could you tell me, in your own words, how you feel about capital punishment?

That completes the interview. Thank you for your cooperation.

Case ID_____                        Respondent's gender:  [ ] Male  [ ] Female

Hello. My name is _____ and I'm conducting a short survey as part of an exercise for my research methods class. Would you be willing to participate in the study? The interview will take less than five minutes. (ENCOURAGE IF RELUCTANT.)

I'm going to read some opinions about the effects of looking at or reading sexual materials such as X-rated magazines and videos. As I read each one, please tell me if you think sexual materials do or do not have that effect. (READ EACH ITEM AND CHECK THE APPROPRIATE CATEGORY.)

|  |  | Yes | No | Don't Know | No Answer |
|---|---|---|---|---|---|
| 1. | Sexual materials provide information about sex. | [ ] | [ ] | [ ] | [ ] |
| 2. | Sexual materials lead to a breakdown of morals. | [ ] | [ ] | [ ] | [ ] |
| 3. | Sexual materials lead people to commit rape. | [ ] | [ ] | [ ] | [ ] |

I am going to name some institutions in this country. As far as the PEOPLE RUNNING these institutions are concerned, would you say that you have a great deal of confidence, only some confidence, or hardly any confidence at all in them? (CODE FOR EACH ITEM; CODE DK FOR "DON'T KNOW" OR NA FOR "NO ANSWER" IF APPROPRIATE.)

|  |  | Great Deal | Only Some | Hardly Any | DK | NA |
|---|---|---|---|---|---|---|
| 4. | Education | [ ] | [ ] | [ ] | [ ] | [ ] |
| 5. | Press | [ ] | [ ] | [ ] | [ ] | [ ] |
| 6. | Congress | [ ] | [ ] | [ ] | [ ] | [ ] |

7. Could you tell me, in your own words, how you feel about capital punishment?

That completes the interview. Thank you for your cooperation.

Case ID_____                    Respondent's gender:  [ ] Male  [ ] Female

Hello. My name is _____ and I'm conducting a short survey as part of an exercise for my research methods class. Would you be willing to participate in the study? The interview will take less than five minutes. (ENCOURAGE IF RELUCTANT.)

I'm going to read some opinions about the effects of looking at or reading sexual materials such as X-rated magazines and videos. As I read each one, please tell me if you think sexual materials do or do not have that effect. (READ EACH ITEM AND CHECK THE APPROPRIATE CATEGORY.)

|  |  | Yes | No | Don't Know | No Answer |
|---|---|---|---|---|---|
| 1. | Sexual materials provide information about sex. | [ ] | [ ] | [ ] | [ ] |
| 2. | Sexual materials lead to a breakdown of morals. | [ ] | [ ] | [ ] | [ ] |
| 3. | Sexual materials lead people to commit rape. | [ ] | [ ] | [ ] | [ ] |

I am going to name some institutions in this country. As far as the PEOPLE RUNNING these institutions are concerned, would you say that you have a great deal of confidence, only some confidence, or hardly any confidence at all in them? (CODE FOR EACH ITEM; CODE DK FOR "DON'T KNOW" OR NA FOR "NO ANSWER" IF APPROPRIATE.)

|  |  | Great Deal | Only Some | Hardly Any | DK | NA |
|---|---|---|---|---|---|---|
| 4. | Education | [ ] | [ ] | [ ] | [ ] | [ ] |
| 5. | Press | [ ] | [ ] | [ ] | [ ] | [ ] |
| 6. | Congress | [ ] | [ ] | [ ] | [ ] | [ ] |

7. Could you tell me, in your own words, how you feel about capital punishment?

That completes the interview. Thank you for your cooperation.

## EXERCISE 9.4                                    Name_____

Develop a questionnaire to be given to students on your campus. Write questions on the following concepts:

1.  Class level
2.  College/division/school (Arts and Science, Business, etc.)
3.  Gender
4.  Attitudes toward gun control (two questions)
5.  Attitudes toward various services provided on your campus (e.g., recreational services, health care, etc.) (three questions)
6.  Number of movies seen
7.  Rating of movie enjoyment
8.  Problems respondents feels are most serious in America today
9.  Attitudes toward one or two political issues that you believe may be relevant to students on your campus (two questions)
10.  Two questions of your choice

Be sure to include instructions, one contingency question, and some matrix questions. Be sure your questionnaire reflects the advice offered in this chapter.

# EXERCISE 9.5                                       Name_____

Review one of the publicly available data sets described in the American Sociological Association Web site (www.asanet.org) or the ICPSR Web site (www.icpsr.umich. edu/) and select one of interest.

1. Describe a study that you could do using this data set. Identify appropriate independent and dependent variables for your study.

2. Assess the validity of the data set that you examined.

# EXERCISE 9.6                              Name_____

Use SPSS or MicroCase (or another data analysis program as indicated by your instructor) to code the questionnaires you completed in Exercise 9.3. Either develop the code categories according to the instructions provided in the chapter or follow your instructor's advice.

Describe any problems you encountered and how you resolved them.

# Chapter 10

## Qualitative Field Research

## OBJECTIVES

1. Define qualitative field research and compare it with other methods.

2. Identify the key strengths of field research.

3. Define and give examples of each of the following elements of social life appropriate for field research: practices, episodes, encounters, roles, relationships, groups, organizations, settlements, social worlds, and lifestyles (or subcultures).

4. Give three examples of research topics particularly appropriate for field research.

5. Compare the various roles the field researcher can assume, ranging from complete participant to complete observer.

6. Note the advantages and disadvantages of adopting the views of the people studied while doing field research.

7. Compare the postures of fully accepting the beliefs, attitudes, and behaviors of those under study versus remaining more "objective."

8. Describe and note the advantages of each of the following field research paradigms: naturalism, ethnomethodology, grounded theory, case studies, the extended case method, institutional ethnography, and participatory action research.

9.  Provide advice on each of the following steps in preparing for the field: review of relevant literature, use of informants, and establishing initial contacts.

10. Provide advice for asking questions in field research, and compare a field research interview with normal conversation.

11. Describe the stages in a complete interviewing process: thematizing, designing, interviewing, transcribing, analyzing, verifying, and reporting.

12. Show how focus groups are relevant in field research.

13. Discuss the strengths and weaknesses of field research, particularly in terms of validity and reliability.

## SUMMARY

Field research closely parallels our daily observation of and participation in social behavior, as well as our attempt to understand such behavior. The social scientific application of field research requires specific skills and techniques and hence is more useful than casual observation. It is both a data-gathering strategy and a theory-generating activity. The term "qualitative field research" is used to distinguish this type of observation method from more quantitative methods (such as surveys).

Field research is particularly appropriate for topics that appear to defy simple quantification and that require the comprehensiveness of perspective the field researcher can provide. It is also useful for studying topics and people within their natural settings and for investigating social processes over time.

The field researcher may investigate various types of social phenomena. One type is practices, which involve behavior. Episodes refer to specific events. Encounters involve people interacting. Roles include positions and behavior. Another type is relationships, which pertain to behavior found in sets of roles. Groups involve small numbers of interacting people. Organizations are larger than groups. Settlements include small-scale "societies." Social worlds reflect ambiguous social entities with vague boundaries and populations. Finally, lifestyles (or subcultures) are examined when field researchers focus on how large numbers of people adjust to life.

The field researcher's role may vary according to the degree of participation. The researcher's identity and purpose are not known to those being observed in the complete participant role. This strategy requires complete adherence to the norms of the group but may involve ethical problems regarding the deception involved in this approach. Also, the researcher may affect what is being studied. The researcher playing the complete observer role observes a social situation without becoming a part of it.

Field researchers are often caught in a dilemma regarding their relations to their subjects. On the one hand, they may choose to actually take on the beliefs, attitudes, and behaviors of those being studied. Doing so enhances insider understanding but comes at the cost of losing the opportunity to see and understand issues within frames of reference unavailable to the subjects. On the other hand, field researchers may choose to remain more distant in their struggle to remain more objective. Assuming both postures yields important advantages.

Several field research paradigms exist. These paradigms do not differ on specific methods used, but they do differ on what the data mean (epistemological differences). Naturalism is an older approach and is based on the positivist notion that social reality "out there," ready to be naturally observed and reported by the researcher as it "really is." The naturalist approach strives to tell people's stories the way they "really are" instead of the way the researchers understands "them." An ethnography is a study that focuses on detailed and accurate description rather than explanation, and is a form of naturalism.

Ethnomethodology is based on the phenomenological premise that reality is socially constructed rather than being "out there" for us to observe. That is, people describe their experiences not "as they are" but "as they make sense of them." Hence, researchers cannot rely on their subjects' stories to depict social realities accurately. Ethnomethodologists study the taken-for-granted expectations that people have about everyday life. One way to study these expectations is to violate the social rules in order to highlight the subtleties of everyday interaction.

Grounded theory is the attempt to derive theories from an analysis of the patterns, themes, and common categories discovered in observational data. It combines a naturalistic approach with a positivist concern for systematic procedures. It allows the researcher to be scientific and creative at the same time.

Case studies focus attention on one or a few instances of some social phenomenon. The term "case" is used broadly. Case studies can be both descriptive and explanatory. The goal can be an idiographic understanding of a particular case or they can help develop more general, nomothetic theories. The extended case method seeks to discover flaws in, and then modifying, existing social theories.

An institutional ethnography examines the ideologies that shape the experiences of oppressed subjects. If researchers ask those in subordinated groups about "how things work," they can discover the institutional practices that shape their realities. This approach helps uncover forms of oppression that often are overlooked by more traditional types of research. Finally, the researcher doing participatory action research serves as a resource to those being studied, typically disadvantaged groups, so that those being studied can act in their own interest. In such studies, those studied play a major role in designing the research to help address their goals.

Field research follows a logical progression of steps. The researcher must first prepare for the field by examining relevant literature, by using informants to help frame the analysis, and by establishing initial contacts with the people to be studied. Field researchers typically employ qualitative interviews to ask questions. This conversational approach yields flexibility in that an answer to one question may influence the next question the researcher wishes to ask. Effective probing is essential. It also helps to assume the role of the "socially acceptable incompetent."

Qualitative interviewing process involves seven stages. Thematizing helps clarify the purpose of the interviews and concepts to be studied. Designing involves laying out the processes of the research. Interviewing involves doing the actual interviews. Transcribing creates a written text. Analyzing determines the meaning of materials gathered relative to the study. Verifying involves checking the reliability and validity of the materials. Finally, through reporting the researcher shares what was learned.

With focus groups, researchers bring people into their study headquarters for qualitative interviewing and observation. A type of group interviewing, the focus group approach is based on structured, semi-structured, or unstructured interviews. It is typically used in marketing research. Typically 12 to 15 people are brought together to engage in a guided discussion of a topic. This method is flexible, has high face validity, produces speedy results, and is inexpensive. But this method also yields less control than when only one person is interviewed, sometimes provides data that are difficult to analyze, requires special skills, sometimes yields problems among groups, involves difficulties in assembling groups, and requires a conducive environment.

The field journal contains the field researcher's observations. Field notes should include both empirical observations as well as interpretations, although the observations and interpretations should be kept separate. Field researchers learn not to trust their memories and hence take many notes at multiple stages in the research process. They record as much as possible so that interpretations that do not seem evident at the time the notes are taken may emerge later.

The greatest strength of the field research method lies in the presence of an observing, thinking researcher on the scene of the action. Field researchers are in a unique position to examine the nuances of attitudes and behaviors and to examine social processes over time; both contribute to a deeper understanding. Field research also is inexpensive and provides a great deal of flexibility for moving between observation and analysis. However, field research seldom yields descriptive statements about large populations because it is a qualitative rather than a quantitative approach. As a result, the field researcher's conclusions are seen as more tentative rather than definitive. Although field research is often more valid than surveys and experiments, it does suffer from lower reliability.

## TERMS

1. case studies
2. extended case method
3. ethnography
4. ethnomethodology
5. focus groups
6. grounded theory
7. institutional ethnography
8. naturalism
9. qualitative field research
10. qualitative interview
11. participatory action research
12. reflexivity
13. symbolic realism

## MATCHING

____ 1. An approach that examines the rules that govern everyday life, often by breaking the rules.

____ 2. An approach based on the assumption that social reality is "out there," ready to be observed and reported by the researcher as it "really is."

____ 3. Deriving theories from an analysis of the patterns, themes, and common categories discovered in observational data.

___ 4. An approach that focuses attention on one or a few instances of some social phenomenon.

___ 5. The purpose of this approach is to discover flaws in, and to modify, existing social theories.

___ 6. An approach in which members of subordinated groups are asked about "how things work" so that researchers can discover the institutional practices that shape their realities.

___ 7. With this paradigm, the researcher's function is to serve as a resource to those being studied, typically disadvantaged groups, as an opportunity for them to act effectively in their own interest.

___ 8. A method in which about 12 to 15 people are brought together to engage in a guided discussion of some topic.

## REVIEW QUESTIONS

1. Field research differs from other modes of observation in that
   a. it is more highly refined.
   b. it is both a data-collecting activity and a theory-generating activity.
   c. it involves more careful conceptualization and operationalization.
   d. it is more dependent on using deduction to generate specific hypotheses for testing.
   e. it is more reliable and valid.

2. Professor Sequoia did a study in which she performed a detailed and accurate description, rather than an explanation, of the social interactions at a church. Which approach did she use?
   a. ethnomethodology
   b. ethnography
   c. participatory action research
   d. focus group
   e. case study

3. Professor Oxley wanted to examine how new teachers make sense of their everyday worlds. He did so by asking some of them to break some rules so that he could better uncover the norms. Which approach did he use?

  a. grounded theory
  b. extended case method
  c. focus group
  d. participatory action research
  e. ethnomethodology

4.  Sonja wanted to do a study of playground interaction among children but, instead of beginning with a theory and developing hypotheses, she wanted to spend a few months observing and then let the patterns or common categories emerge. Which approach did she use?
    a. ethnography
    b. naturalism
    c. qualitative interviews
    d. grounded theory
    e. focus group

5.  Professor Sullivan performed an observational study of the norms that govern interactions between cab drivers and their passengers. Which one of the following does this example reflect?
    a. roles
    b. encounters
    c. episodes
    d. groups
    e. settlements

6.  The most serious ethical problems exist for which type of research role?
    a. complete participant
    b. participant-as-observer
    c. observer-as-participant
    d. complete observer
    e. ethnographer

7.  A common first step in doing field research is
    a. considering ethics.
    b. forming a hypothesis.
    c. constructing a theory.
    d. deciding on level of participation.
    e. reviewing literature.

8. Which one of the following is most appropriate for asking questions during field research?
   a. structured questionnaire
   b. unstructured questionnaire
   c. structured interviews
   d. qualitative interviews
   e. projective techniques

9. Which one of the following is *false* regarding field notes? Or are they all true?
   a. Don't trust your memory more than you have to.
   b. Take notes in stages.
   c. Get the major points, but don't worry about getting as many details as you can.
   d. Rewrite your notes before going to sleep.
   e. All are true.

10. Professor Patecki studied a ghetto in a big city as part of his field research. Which element did he study?
    a. practices
    b. lifestyles
    c. settlement
    d. relationships
    e. episodes

11. Professor Johnson wants to ask members of a subordinated group about how things work in their lives so that he can identify the structural practices that shape their realities. Which approach is best?
    a. institutional ethnography
    b. focus group.
    c. extended case method
    d. participatory action research
    e. ethnography

12. Francesca wanted to study homeless women, but in a way that allowed the homeless women to define the research problem, define the remedies desired, and take the lead in designing the research that will help them realize their aims. Which approach should she use?
    a. participatory action research
    b. case study
    c. extended case method
    d. grounded theory

e. naturalism

13. In comparison to surveys and experiments, field research has
    a. high validity and high reliability.
    b. high validity and low reliability.
    c. low validity and low reliability.
    d. low validity and high reliability.
    e. high reliability, but only when the validity is high.

## DISCUSSION QUESTIONS

1. Explain what Babbie means when he says that field research is not only a data-gathering activity but a theory-generating activity as well. Illustrate each function. Which is more important? Why?

2. Compare and contrast the types of qualitative inquiry: naturalism, ethnomethodology, grounded theory, case studies, the extended case method, institutional ethnography, and participatory action research.. Select a topic and show how this topic would be studied with each approach.

3.  Babbie discusses the following stages in field research: preparation for the field, asking questions, focus groups, and recording observations. Select three and discuss the basic principles involved for effectively completing each.

4.  Compare the strengths and weaknesses of field research with both surveys and experiments, particularly in terms of reliability and validity.

# EXERCISE 10.1

Name_____

Your assignment is to observe and understand the social dynamics of jaywalking—defined narrowly for our purposes as "pedestrians crossing the street against the light at intersections."

You are to make three separate observations of at least 15 minutes duration each.

Your specific tasks are to discover:

1.  What are the characteristics of people who are the most likely to jaywalk and what are the characteristics of those least likely to jaywalk?

2.  What are the characteristics of people who are likely to stimulate jaywalking by others? That is, what are the characteristics of those, when they jaywalk, who seem to be followed by people who were previously waiting for the light to change?

Record your field notes below.

Please don't get arrested for jaywalking!

FIELD NOTES:

# EXERCISE 10.2                         Name_____

Your assignment is to pick some location or situation in which strangers are put in physical proximity to one another for a period of time. Examples include a bus stop, a table at the library, a train station or airport waiting room, a hospital waiting room, a party, etc.

Observe at your location for at least an hour. Examine the ways in which strangers interact with one another. Notice the ways in which they communicate: through words, facial expressions, body postures, and the like. Examine what is communicated, in what situations, with what effect, and by what kinds of people. Examine also the importance of social space and physical space. Pay special attention to (a) the varieties in all these things, and (b) any regular patterns that seem to exist.

Record your field notes below.

FIELD NOTES:

## EXERCISE 10.3

Name_____

Your assignment is to plan a possible field research project to investigate differences in friendship patterns in coed and single-sex residence halls. The questions below deal with some of the concepts you may wish to consider in such a study. For each, describe some of the possible indicators that might be relevant to the concept. You can observe and you can do interviews using a field notebook, but you cannot hand out a questionnaire or do formal interviews using structured interview schedules. You want to be able to determine if the friendships are with people in the same dorm.

1. How would you determine the number of friendships each resident in the coed and single-sex residence halls has (friendships in the same hall in which the resident lives)?

2. How would you determine the quality of friendships? Think of quality as the "strength" or "intensity" of friendship. How would you determine if the friendships are close (strong), distant (weak), or in between?

3. Which other aspects of friendship patterns would you expect to differ in the two situations? List at least three along with possible indicators. Think about such activities as dating, recreation, visiting, topics of conversation, and the like, but be sure to be specific and describe how you would expect them to differ in the two types of dorms and what would be some indicators that you could observe to determine if they do differ.

(continued)

4. List two other variables that you might consider in a study such as this. These should be variables besides residence hall type that might be related to the number and quality of friendships that develop. Think about what might be some variables that would determine whom residents become friends with or determine how strong a friendship would develop.

5. Describe how you might measure the first variable you noted in #4. What would you be looking for, or what types of questions might you ask?

6. Describe how you might measure the second variable in #4. What would you be looking for or what types of questions might you ask?

# EXERCISE 10.4

Name_____

Review either or both of the following Web sites on qualitative analysis and find a field research study:

qualitative-research.net/fqs/fqs-eng.htm
www.ualberta.ca/~jrnorris/qual.html

1. Summarize the study.


2. Which of the following are represented in the study: naturalism, ethnomethodology, grounded theory, case studies, the extended case method, institutional ethnography, and participatory action research? Explain how.


3. Which of the following elements of social life are examined in the study: practices, episodes, encounters, roles, relationships, groups, organizations, settlements, social worlds, and lifestyles (or subcultures)? Explain.

(continued)

4. How were the data analyzed? Present the major conclusions.

5. Address any ethical issues that emerged.

6. Explain why the field research method was the most appropriate method to use for this study.

# Chapter 11

## Unobtrusive Research

## OBJECTIVES

1. Describe and compare the three unobtrusive research designs: content analysis, analysis of existing statistics, and historical/comparative analysis.

2. Give three examples of artifacts that content analysts might study.

3. Give three examples of content analysis in which the unit of observation differs from the unit of analysis.

4. Show how the unit of analysis influences sample selection in content analysis.

5. Illustrate how a researcher might employ each of the following sampling techniques in content analysis: simple random sampling, systematic sampling, stratified sampling, and cluster sampling.

6. Differentiate manifest content from latent content by definition and example.

7. Present advice for the development of code categories in content analysis.

8. Present advice for counting and record keeping in content analysis.

9. Outline the strengths and weaknesses of content analysis.

10. Explain how analytic induction is used in qualitative content analysis.

11. Summarize the difficulties with units of analysis in existing statistics.

12. Explain why validity is a problem with existing statistics, and present two strategies for resolving this problem.

13. Explain why reliability is a problem with existing statistics, and present two strategies for resolving this problem.

14. List three sources of existing statistics.

15. List three sources of data for historical/comparative analysis.

16. Discuss the role of corroboration in enhancing the quality of existing statistics.

17. Discuss the role of verstehen, and ideal types in the analysis of existing statistics.


## SUMMARY

Unlike other methods, unobtrusive methods do not generally influence the data gathered. Content analysis is one type of unobtrusive method. It may be applied to virtually any form of communication and involves examining artifacts to answer the classic question: "Who says what, to whom, how, and with what effect?"

The complexity of units of analysis is very apparent in content analysis, particularly when the unit of observation differs from the unit of analysis. Content analysts must address this issue directly because sample selection depends largely on the unit of analysis. Any of the conventional sampling techniques described in Chapter 8 may be employed in content analysis, including random or systematic sampling, stratified sampling, and cluster sampling. Sampling need not end when the researcher reaches the unit of analysis.

Content analysts distinguish manifest from latent content. Manifest content is the visible surface content, and its coding approximates the use of a standardized questionnaire. Latent content reflects the underlying meaning, but this advantage comes at a cost of reliability and specificity. It is best to code both types.

Conceptualization plays a key role in determining code categories and frequently requires both inductive and deductive methods. Attributes of variables must be clearly specified, and each of the several levels of measurement may be employed. The coding operations must be amenable to data processing. Hence, the final product must be numerical, units of analysis and units of observation must be clearly distinguished, and the base from which counting is done must be carefully considered and must be presented. Occasionally a qualitative analysis of the materials is more appropriate. Analytic induction can be used for this purpose; it begins with observations to develop hypotheses but goes beyond description to uncover patterns and relationships among variables. The main danger in this procedure is that the researcher may misclassify observations to support emerging hypotheses.

The greatest advantage of content analysis is economy in terms of time and energy. Content analysis is also quite safe—mistakes can be easily rectified and the study redone. Content analysis also allows the study of processes over time. Finally, content analysis is unobtrusive. But it is limited to an examination of recorded communications. Content analysis has both advantages and disadvantages in terms of validity and reliability.

Many governmental and other agencies collect official or quasi-official statistics. Existing statistics can provide the main data for a social scientific study and can also provide supplemental sources of data for studies employing other research designs. The unit of analysis is frequently not the individual but instead is found in different types of aggregates. The aggregate nature of existing statistics sometimes presents a problem, requiring the social scientist to make inferences from one level to another. Doing so, however, may result in committing the ecological fallacy—generalizing from data gathered at one unit of analysis to another unit of analysis.

Existing statistics are particularly prone to problems of validity because the data may not reflect a particular measure that a social scientist has constructed. This problem may be addressed through logical reasoning and replication. Reliability may also be a problem because different agencies use different data-gathering strategies with varying levels of accuracy. This problem may be addressed through awareness and logical reasoning, as well as replication. There are many sources of existing statistics, such as *The Statistical Abstract of the United States, The Demographic Yearbook*, and Web sites for various governmental agencies.

Historical/comparative research helps trace the development of social forms over time and helps compare such developments across cultures. In its purest form, this approach relies on "primary sources" of data, such as diaries and official government documents. Once again, problems of reliability and bias enter, which again can be addressed through replication (known as corroboration in historical research).

Analysts in this tradition often stress the role of *verstehen*, an understanding of the essential quality of a social phenomenon. Sometimes ideal types help researchers find patterns in the details of their data; ideal types are conceptual models composed of the essential characteristics of social. Historical/comparative research is often performed in light of a particular theoretical paradigm, such as Marxism. Time-series data can be used to do a quantitative analysis of changing conditions over time.

## TERMS

1. analysis of existing statistics
2. analytic induction
3. coding
4. content analysis
5. corroboration
6. ecological fallacy
7. historical/comparative analysis
8. ideal types
9. latent content
10. manifest content
11. unobtrusive measures
12. *verstehen*

## MATCHING

___  1.  A research method in which a class of social artifacts is analyzed.

___  2.  The visible, surface content of a communication.

___  3.  The underlying meaning of a communication.

___  4.  This occurs when a researcher gathers data from groups and generalizes to individuals.

___  5.  In historical research the process by which several sources point to the same set of "facts."

___  6.  Research methods that allow the researcher to study social life from afar, without influencing it in the process.

___  7.  Experiential understanding of social life.

___  8.  Conceptual models composed of the essential characteristics of social phenomena.

## REVIEW QUESTIONS

1. Content analysis may be applied to
   a. anything that is written.
   b. any form of communication.
   c. anything social scientific that does not involve surveys, experiments, or observation.
   d. anything that has both manifest and latent content.
   e. anything that involves statistics.

2. Sampling and data analysis are generally more complex in content analysis because
   a. the method is less highly developed than other modes of observation.
   b. both sampling and data analysis are not as appropriate.
   c. sampling error cannot be calculated.
   d. current statistical techniques do not apply.
   e. the units of analysis are not always clear.

3. Which of the following sampling techniques is/are applicable in content analysis?
   a. simple random
   b. systematic
   c. stratified
   d. purposive
   e. all of the above

4. Professor Hague codes the number of times the word sex is used in commercials. She is examining
   a. latent structure.
   b. ecological fallacy.
   c. manifest content.
   d. corroboration.
   e. latent content.

5. Professor Spykes codes how frequently situation comedies portray sexual activities. He is examining
   a. latent structure.
   b. sociometric choices.
   c. manifest content.
   d. corroboration.
   e. latent content.

6. Which one of the following is *not* a strength of content analysis? Or are they all strengths?
    a. economy in time and money
    b. flexibility and safety
    c. allows study of process over time
    d. unobtrusive
    e. all are strengths

7. In studying suicide, Durkheim used
    a. surveys.
    b. experiments.
    c. observation.
    d. government statistics.
    e. evaluation research.

8. Durkheim concluded that suicides are a product of
    a. social instability and disintegration.
    b. temperature and population density.
    c. political party structure.
    d. education and family structure.
    e. depression.

9. The most common unit of analysis involved in the analysis of existing statistics is
    a. individuals.
    b. groups.
    c. organizations.
    d. artifacts.
    e. cities.

10. Because most existing statistics are aggregated, researchers must avoid the error of
    a. overgeneralizing.
    b. validity.
    c. drawing conclusions about individuals.
    d. drawing conclusions about the aggregate.
    e. reductionism.

11. A *major* disadvantage of analyzing existing data is
    a. ethical violations.

   b. errors in coding.
   c. inappropriate statistical techniques.
   d. inappropriate units of analysis.
   e. validity of measures.

12. The two features of science used to handle the problem of validity in analysis of existing statistics are
   a. cumulativeness and generalizability.
   b. generalizability and objectivity.
   c. objectivity and replication.
   d. replication and logical reasoning.
   e. logical reasoning and cumulativeness.

13. One of the most valuable sources of existing statistics is
   a. *Statistical Abstract of the United States.*
   b. Superintendent of Documents.
   c. *TV Guide.*
   d. *World Book Encyclopedia.*
   e. Gallup polls.

14. Professor Dealy performed his historical analysis of race relations over the last 100 years and is now at work developing a conceptual model composed of the essential characteristics of racism. He detailed the core features of racism in his attempt to create a theoretical model of "perfect" racism. He used which one of the following?
   a. hermeneutics
   b. ideal type formation
   c. *verstehen*
   d. sociological historical analysis
   e. paradigm development

## DISCUSSION QUESTIONS

1. Compare and contrast content analysis, analysis of existing statistics, and historical/comparative analysis in terms of purposes, strengths, and weaknesses.

2. Explain why units of analysis are of particular concern in content analysis.

3. Explain why social science researchers are interested in both manifest and latent content. Show how these two types of content are both similar and different.

4. Discuss the special problems regarding validity and reliability experienced by those who analyze existing statistics.

# EXERCISE 11.1

Name_____

You are to compare three national news magazines in their coverage of some major news story in the past year.

1.  First, select a news story that involved different points of view. Note the story here.

2.  Next, select three news magazines, from among such publications as *Newsweek*, *Time*, *U.S. News & World Report*, *The New Republic*, *The Nation*, *National Review*, etc. (Your instructor may suggest others.) Pick two different issues of each magazine. Indicate the magazines and the dates of the issues you studied.

Magazine 1 _____
    Date of first issue studied: _____
    Date of second issue studied: _____

Magazine 2 _____
    Date of first issue studied: _____
    Date of second issue studied: _____

Magazine 3 _____
    Date of first issue studied: _____
    Date of second issue studied: _____

3.  Describe the method you used to determine the relative amount of coverage each magazine devoted to the story you are studying.

(continued)

4. Report your findings regarding the amount of coverage each magazine devoted to the issue. Provide both data tabulations and your interpretations of those data.

    Magazine # 1:

    Magazine # 2:

    Magazine # 3:

5. Describe the method you used to determine the editorial positions taken by the magazines.

6. Report your findings regarding the editorial positions taken by the three magazines. Provide both data tabulations and your interpretations of those data.

    Magazine # 1:

    Magazine # 2:

    Magazine # 3:

# EXERCISE 11.2

Name_____

This exercise involves examining television commercials. Select three commercials for analysis. If feasible, record them so you can review them again. Try to pick commercials that have appeared repeatedly. Examine them for their manifest and latent content.

For additional information on video content analysis, see www.lienhart.de/VCAHome /index.html.

1. Describe the commercials before beginning your analysis.

   Commercial # 1:

   Commercial # 2:

   Commercial # 3:

2. Describe how you assessed the manifest content of each commercial and summarize the manifest content for each.

   Commercial # 1:

(continued)

Commercial # 2:

Commercial # 3:

3.  Describe how you assessed the latent content of each commercial and summarize the latent content for each.

    Commercial # 1:

    Commercial # 2:

    Commercial # 3:

# EXERCISE 11.3

Name_____

Test the following hypothesis: States with large populations have higher auto theft rates than do states with small populations.

To test this hypothesis, you must determine the population of each of the 50 states in a recent year and the number of auto thefts reported in each state that year. You might check the *Statistical Abstract of the United States* (www.census.gov/statab/ www/).

Complete the worksheet below, and rank order the 50 states in terms of population. Combine them into five groups of ten each, ranging from the ten smallest to the ten largest. Once you have them in groups of ten, combine the population for each group, combine the total number of thefts for each group, and divide the combined number of thefts by the combined population to get the auto theft rate for each group (see step 3).

1.  Give the bibliographical citation of the source(s) from which your data are taken.

2.  Complete the following worksheet:

|  | POPU-LATION | AUTO THEFTS |  | POPU-LATION | AUTO THEFTS |
|---|---|---|---|---|---|
| Alabama | ____ | ____ | Connecticut | ____ | ____ |
| Alaska | ____ | ____ | Delaware | ____ | ____ |
| Arizona | ____ | ____ | Florida | ____ | ____ |
| Arkansas | ____ | ____ | Georgia | ____ | ____ |
| California | ____ | ____ | Hawaii | ____ | ____ |
| Colorado | ____ | ____ | Idaho | ____ | ____ |

(continued)

| | | | | | |
|---|---|---|---|---|---|
| Illinois | ___ | ___ | New York | ___ | ___ |
| Indiana | ___ | ___ | North Carolina | ___ | ___ |
| Iowa | ___ | ___ | North Dakota | ___ | ___ |
| Kansas | ___ | ___ | Ohio | ___ | ___ |
| Kentucky | ___ | ___ | Oklahoma | ___ | ___ |
| Louisiana | ___ | ___ | Oregon | ___ | ___ |
| Maine | ___ | ___ | Pennsylvania | ___ | ___ |
| Maryland | ___ | ___ | Rhode Island | ___ | ___ |
| Massachusetts | ___ | ___ | South Carolina | ___ | ___ |
| Michigan | ___ | ___ | South Dakota | ___ | ___ |
| Minnesota | ___ | ___ | Tennessee | ___ | ___ |
| Mississippi | ___ | ___ | Texas | ___ | ___ |
| Missouri | ___ | ___ | Utah | ___ | ___ |
| Montana | ___ | ___ | Vermont | ___ | ___ |
| Nebraska | ___ | ___ | Virginia | ___ | ___ |
| Nevada | ___ | ___ | Washington | ___ | ___ |
| New Hampshire | ___ | ___ | West Virginia | ___ | ___ |
| New Jersey | ___ | ___ | Wisconsin | ___ | ___ |
| New Mexico | ___ | ___ | Wyoming | ___ | ___ |

(continued)

3. Complete the following table (warning: be sure to convert states' auto theft *rates* into *numbers* of auto thefts per state before combining state figures):

|  | COMBINED POPULATION | COMBINED NUMBER OF AUTO THEFTS | COMBINED AUTO THEFT RATE |
|---|---|---|---|
| Smallest ten states | _____ | _____ | _____ |
| Second smallest ten states | _____ | _____ | _____ |
| Third smallest ten states | _____ | _____ | _____ |
| Fourth smallest ten states | _____ | _____ | _____ |
| Largest ten states | _____ | _____ | _____ |

4. Give a brief research report, indicating whether you feel the hypothesis was confirmed or disconfirmed.

# EXERCISE 11.4                              Name_____

Select a recent article reporting on content analysis research (see www.content-analysis.de or garnet.acns.fsu.edu/~jbm4162/content.html).

1.  Summarize the article.



2.  Show how the study reflects three points Babbie makes about content analy-sis.



3.  Assess the quality of the study.

# EXERCISE 11.5

Name_____

Assess the General Social Survey (see Appendix 1) in terms of Babbie's discussion of the issues important to consider when using existing statistics.

216

# Chapter 12

## Evaluation Research

## OBJECTIVES

1. Identify the purposes of evaluation research.

2. Identify three factors influencing the growth of evaluation research.

3. Define and illustrate social intervention.

4. Describe why it is important to identify the purpose of an intervention.

5. Define and illustrate the outcome (or response) variable.

6. Give three examples of experimental contexts that may influence specific evaluation research studies.

7. Describe two problems with specifying interventions.

8. Explain why it is important to define the population of possible subjects for whom the program is appropriate.

9. Compare the two options for measuring variables.

10. Provide advice for operationalizing success or failure of an intervention.

11. Apply the classical experimental design to an evaluation research study.

12. Define quasi-experimental designs.

13. Define and illustrate time-series designs.

14. Define and illustrate nonequivalent control groups designs.

15. Define and illustrate multiple time-series designs.

16. Define and illustrate cost-benefit analysis.

17. Show how evaluation research can be less structured and more qualitative.

18. Discuss why evaluation research is particularly subject to problems in the actual execution of the research.

19. Summarize three reasons why the implications of evaluation research are not always put into practice.

20. Define and illustrate social indicators research.

21. Define and illustrate computer simulation.

## SUMMARY

Evaluation research employs the same research methods described in previous chapters. Its uniqueness lies in its purpose: to evaluate the impact of social interventions. It has experienced increased popularity due to the desire of social scientists to influence the quality of life as well as to increased federal requirements for program evaluation and the availability of research funds to meet those requirements.

Several topics are addressed with evaluation research. Critically important is a clear specification of both the purpose of the intervention to be evaluated as well as the measurement of the key variables. Researchers commonly specify different aspects of desired outcomes and allow for varying levels of success in meeting program objectives. The context within which the study occurs is critical, and hence these variables must be identified and measured as well. Extraneous variables must also be considered. Evaluation researchers must carefully identify the population of possible subjects for the study and must decide whether to create new measures or use existing measures.

Perhaps the most critical aspect of evaluation research is determining whether the program being studied succeeded or failed. Researchers typically allow for gradations of success or failure and frequently employ cost-benefit analysis to determine benefits relative to costs. But researchers find it difficult to assign exact dollar values. Measurement decisions are complicated by both practical and political considerations because evaluation researchers must work with the people responsible for the program that is being evaluated.

Some evaluation research studies employ the classical experimental design, in which subjects are randomly assigned to experimental and control groups. However, most evaluation research studies cannot meet the demands of random assignment and hence employ quasi-experiments. Time-series designs examine processes occurring over time. Nonequivalent control groups designs are used when an existing "control" group appears similar to the experimental group. Multiple time-series designs are an improved version of the nonequivalent control groups design and employ more than one time-series analysis. Evaluation research need not always be quantitative; less structured and more qualitative evaluation research studies help provide an in-depth understanding of processes producing the observed results.

In comparison to the traditional designs, evaluation research is prone to several types of problems. Logistical problems emerge because evaluation researchers often lack sufficient control over the design in real-life contexts. Researchers must also deal with reluctant and counterproductive administrators who wish to protect favorite programs. Social interventions frequently raise ethical issues, particularly regarding who receives and does not receive what type of stimulus. Political and ideological issues can also intrude.

Evaluation research is designed to be used to make a difference in the execution of some program. Results of evaluation research studies frequently contradict popular beliefs or personal beliefs of administrators involved. Evaluation researchers themselves often fail to present the implications of their research in a way that nonresearchers can understand. Sometimes, however, implications of evaluation studies are taken seriously, as demonstrated by the Manhattan Bail Bond project.

The use of social indicators has increased in recent years as a nonexperimental form of evaluation research. The use of such indicators makes it possible to monitor many aspects of social life on a large scale. With computer simulation, evaluation researchers can develop mathematical equations describing the relationships that link social variables to one another. By varying one or more of the variables in the equation, social scientists can examine the implications of specific changes.

## TERMS

1. applied research
2. computer simulation
3. cost-benefit analysis
4. evaluation research
5. experimental contexts
6. multiple time-series designs
7. nonequivalent control group design
8. outcome/response variable
9. quasi-experiments
10. social intervention
11. social indicators
12. time-series designs
13. vested interests

## MATCHING

___ 1. Experiments that lack random assignment subjects to experimental and control groups.

___ 2. The variable that reflects the result of an intervention.

___ 3. A type of quasi-experimental design that uses a comparison group rather than a control group to which subjects are randomly assigned.

___ 4. Aspects of societies that are monitored.

___ 5. Ego involvement in a project that often hampers the implementation of evaluation research results.

___ 6. A form of applied research that assesses the impact of social interventions.

___ 7. The general class of research that is intended to have some real-world effect.

___ 8. Variables external to the experiment itself, yet affecting it.

## REVIEW QUESTIONS

1. Evaluation research employs which method(s)?
   a. surveys

    b. experiments
    c. observation
    d. existing statistics
    e. all of the above

2. Which one of the following is *correct*?
    a. Evaluation research is a form of program evaluation.
    b. Evaluation research is a form of applied research.
    c. Applied research is a form of evaluation research.
    d. Applied research is a form of program evaluation.
    e. Program evaluation is a form of survey research.

3. The recent growth of evaluation research is due primarily to
    a. increased methodological sophistication.
    b. the spurt in the number of social scientists.
    c. increased federal requirements and financial support.
    d. disagreement over policy implications.
    e. the decline in quality of services rendered by social service agencies.

4. Which one of the following is an example of a program intervention?
    a. a study of dating behavior among college students
    b. a study of the effect of gender on participation in voluntary associations
    c. a study of the effect of religiosity on income
    d. a study of the effect of team teaching on learning
    e. a study of the effect of organizational size on productivity

5. The *most* critical problem in evaluation research is
    a. dealing with ethical issues.
    b. measuring the outcome.
    c. developing an adequate sample.
    d. dealing with political constraints.
    e. developing appropriate statistical techniques.

6. Which of the following strategies is particularly useful for measuring the effects of experimental contexts?
    a. multiple regression
    b. multiple indicators
    c. involving clients
    d. blind designs
    e. control groups

7. The advantage in using measures that have been used previously is that they have
    a. greater conceptual diversity.
    b. known dimensionality.
    c. known degrees of validity and reliability.
    d. greater statistical rigor.
    e. more policy implications.

8. Quasi-experimental designs differ from "true" experimental designs
    a. by shorter duration and more political constraints.
    b. by more political constraints and more ethical considerations.
    c. by more ethical considerations and lack of random assignment.
    d. by lack of random assignment and lack of a control group.
    e. by lack of a control group and shorter duration.

9. Professor Gabino wants to do an evaluation research study on the effect of a new treatment for learning disabilities. She has only one group of clients and wants to assess the effects over the course of a couple of months. Which design would be best?
    a. classical
    b. nonequivalent control group
    c. time-series
    d. posttest-only control group design
    e. factorial

10. Professor Yee wants to do an evaluation study of the effects of a patient education program on patient anxiety. He uses one wing in a hospital for the experiment and compares the results with a similar group of patients in a similar wing in another hospital. Which design would be best?
    a. classical
    b. nonequivalent control group
    c. time-series
    d. posttest-only control group design
    e. factorial

11. Cost-benefit analysis is used to assess
    a. the long-term effect on clients.
    b. the cost of the experiment relative to the social scientific knowledge gained.
    c. how much of an increase of effect is sufficient for success, given cost.
    d. the costs to society relative to the benefits to the clients.
    e. the costs of the program relative to the number of staff hours invested.

12. Evaluation researchers encounter more logistical problems than other researchers because evaluation research
    a. occurs in the context of real life.
    b. takes longer.
    c. is more costly.
    d. has more measurement problems.
    e. examines more variables.

13. The ethical issues of evaluation research center on
    a. the policy implications.
    b. the administrators of the agency.
    c. the nature of the clients.
    d. the nature of the social intervention.
    e. informed consent.

14. Computer simulation is particularly useful for
    a. measuring social indicators.
    b. analyzing many variables.
    c. outlining policy implications.
    d. improving reliability and validity.
    e. predicting outcomes of specific social changes.

## DISCUSSION QUESTIONS

1. Discuss why measurement is important in evaluation research. Describe the role of measurement in each of the four types of variables Babbie discusses.

2. Explain why evaluation researchers find it difficult to employ the classical experimental design, which is best suited to establishing causality. Which designs are more typically used? Why?

3. What are the major reasons why evaluation research results are often ignored? What could be done to remedy this situation?

4. Discuss some of the ethical problems that are particularly troublesome in doing evaluation research. Examine strategies for addressing these problems.

5. Economists have developed a substantial number of indicators to monitor the country's economic health (consumer price index, unemployment rate, and others), many of which are a part of the daily news. How would you explain the scarcity of noneconomic social indicators in the coverage of social issues?

## EXERCISE 12.1                         Name_____

The purpose of this workbook is to give you some firsthand experience in applying the various aspects of social research, on the assumption that you will learn research methods better that way. The purpose of this workbook, then, is to assist you in understanding the various aspects of social research. In this exercise, you are to design an evaluation study to determine the effectiveness of this workbook. You are planning your project now for implementation next year. So you have some control over the setting in creating your design.

Describe all aspects of your study design, including the likely conclusions.

1.  Give specific information regarding the following types of variables: outcomes, experimental contexts, intervention, population, new versus existing measures, and determining success/failure. How will you address and/or measure each?

   Outcomes:

   Experimental contexts:

   Intervention:

   Population:

   New versus existing measures:

   Success or failure:

(continued)

2.  Describe which design you selected and why. Outline the study in detail using this design.

3.  Describe possible logistical and ethical problems and how you would handle them.

4.  Present some fake data and interpret the results.

# EXERCISE 12.2                          Name_____

You are to design an evaluation research study. Find a newspaper (see www.newspap erlinks.com for links to newspapers on line. Find a report of some innovative social program, such as prison reform, a program to provide jobs to young people during school vacations, or a proposal for a new welfare system. Or simply select an innovative social program you are interested in if your instructor so advises. Describe how you would evaluate the success of the program.

1. Briefly describe the innovative program.

2. Specify the key dependent variable that is influenced by the program.

3. Describe as specifically as possible how you would measure that dependent variable.

(continued)

4.  How would you design and conduct your evaluation of the program? Be sure to describe any ways in which the program itself would have to be modified in order to permit your evaluation. Also, specify the data you would need to collect.

5.  Write a hypothetical research report, reporting the "results" of your evaluation of the program. Make up data, and be sure to give your conclusion about the program's success or failure, along with reasons for this conclusion.

# EXERCISE 12.3

Name_____

You have been asked to develop a composite measure of the quality of life on your campus.

1. Outline the social indicators you would use to develop such a measure. Be specific. Explain why you selected these indicators.

2. Now suppose data on your social indicators have been collected over a ten-year period. What might you be able to do with these data?

# EXERCISE 12.4

Name_____

Visit one of the following Web sites and locate a topic of interest (or consult other sites noted in Appendix B in the text):

www.lib.umich.edu/libhome/Documents.center/stsoc.html
www.whitehouse.gov/fsbr/ssbr.html

1. Describe how the statistics reported on your topic reflect social indicators research.

2. What can you conclude about your topic? If the data span several years, note any changes over time.

# Part 4

## Analysis of Data

# Chapter 13

## Qualitative Data Analysis

## OBJECTIVES

1.  Define and illustrate qualitative analysis.

2.  Compare the connection between data analysis and theory in both qualitative research and quantitative research.

3.  Illustrate these ways of looking for patterns in a particular research topic: frequencies, magnitudes, structures, processes, causes, and consequences.

4.  Compare the two strategies of cross-case analysis: variable-oriented analysis and case-oriented analysis.

5.  Describe the four stages of the constant comparative method used in the grounded theory method.

6.  Define and illustrate semiotics.

7.  Define and illustrate conversation analysis.

8.  Show how coding works in qualitative analysis.

9.  Explain why standardization is a key principle in quantitative analysis but not so in qualitative analysis.

10. Define open coding.

11. Summarize the role of memoing in qualitative data analysis and compare these types: code notes, theoretical notes, and operational notes.

12. Compare these types of memos: elemental, sorting, and integrating.

13. Explain the role of concept mapping.

14. Show how computers can be used in qualitative data analysis.

15. Illustrate how the qualitative analysis of quantitative data is useful.

## SUMMARY

Quantitative analysis of social research data is the most dominant approach in the social sciences. Its emphasis on statistical analysis, however, sometimes conceals another very useful approach to making sense of social observations: qualitative analysis. Qualitative data analysis include methods for examining and making sense of social research data without converting them to a numerical format. It is easy to lose sight of theory in quantitative data analysis. In qualitative data analysis, however, data collection, analysis, and theory are more closely connected.

The approach to theory used in qualitative data analysis can best be described as a process of looking for plausible relationships proposed among concepts and sets of concepts. Discovering patterns lies at the root of this explanatory focus, which can be done by looking at different analytical topics. Frequencies simply measure how often something occurs. Magnitudes reflect the levels of particular variables. Structures reflect different types of a variable. Processes reflect an order among the elements of structure. Causes are the factors influencing something of interest. Consequences are the outcomes of a particular variable.

Qualitative data analysts look for patterns appearing across several observations that usually represent different cases under study, known as cross-case analysis. Two types of cross-case analysis can be used. Variable-oriented analysis examines the impact of several independent variables on a particular dependent variable across many cases. Case-oriented analysis, on the other hand, involves looking deeply at one or just a few cases. The researcher may see the critical elements of one subject's experiences as instances of more general social concepts or variables.

The Grounded Theory Method stresses the importance of establishing theories on an inductive basis. This approach begins with observations instead of hypotheses and discovers patterns and develops theories from the ground up, with no preconceptions. The Grounded Theory Method uses the constant comparative method, which includes four stages. The first compares incidents applicable to each category. The second integrates categories and their properties. The third delimits the theory, and the fourth writes the theory.

Semiotics is the science of signs and addresses symbols and meanings. Those following this approach stress that meanings attached to signs are socially constructed. Signs are any things that are assigned special meanings. Conversation analysis examines closely the ways people converse with each other in order to uncover the implicit assumptions and structures in social life. It is based on three assumptions. First, conversation is a socially structured activity. Second, conversations must be understood contextually. Third, detailed transcriptions of conversations are required to understand the meaning and structure of conversation.

Qualitative data processing brings order to qualitative data. Coding is central and involves  classifying or categorizing pieces of data. Coding in qualitative data processing centers on the concept as the organizing principle. This differs from the emphasis on a standardized unit of analysis in more statistical analyses. Qualitative data analysis involves open coding, the naming and categorizing of phenomena through close examination of data. This important first step yields clues for identifying similarities and differences and helps uncover people's assumptions.

As qualitative data analysts code data, they often use the technique of memoing– writing notes to yourself and others involved in the project. Three types of memos are used in the Grounded Theory Method. Code notes identify the code labels and their meanings. Theoretical notes address the meanings of concepts, relationships among concepts, and theoretical propositions. Operational notes address methodological issues, such as data collection circumstances. Other types of memos can be used nearer the final writing stage. The elemental memo is a detailed analytic rendering of some relatively specific matter. The sorting memo presents key themes in the analysis and is based on several elemental memos. The integrating memo ties together the various sorting memos and brings order to the analytical phase of the project. Sometimes qualitative data analysts portray their concepts in a graphical format, which helps identify relationships among concepts more clearly. Various computer programs have greatly simplified qualitative data analysis. Finally, qualitative data analysis of quantitative data often yields new insights and shows how the two approaches are not incompatible.

## TERMS

| | | | |
|---|---|---|---|
| 1. | case-oriented analysis | 10. | integrating memo |
| 2. | code notes | 11. | memoing |
| 3. | coding | 12. | open coding |
| 4. | concept mapping | 13. | operational notes |
| 5. | constant comparative method | 14. | qualitative analysis |
| 6. | conversation analysis | 15. | semiotics |
| 7. | cross-case analysis | 16. | sorting memo |
| 8. | elemental memo | 17. | theoretical notes |
| 9. | Grounded Theory Method | 18. | variable-oriented analysis |

## MATCHING

___ 1. The type of cross-case analysis that focuses on interrelationships among variables.

___ 2. A method for building theories on an inductive basis that begins with observations rather than hypotheses and seeks to discover patterns.

___ 3. The process of classifying or categorizing individual pieces of data.

___ 4. A type of memoing in which the researcher reflects on the meanings of concepts, relationships among concepts, and theoretical propositions.

___ 5. The type of memo which presents key themes in the analysis and is based on several elemental memos.

___ 6. Putting concepts in a graphical format to enable the researcher to think out the relationships among concepts more clearly.

___ 7. Methods for examining social research data without converting them to a numerical format.

___ 8. The type of cross-case analysis that involves looking more closely into a few particular cases.

# REVIEW QUESTIONS

1. Professor Martini has done a qualitative analysis of fraternity parties. He selected one party for intensive analysis of the social interactions that occur between women and men. He is using which method?
   a. variable-oriented analysis
   b. memoing
   c. open coding
   d. case-oriented analysis
   e. operational notes

2. Martini then compared incidents at various parties applicable to his categories of analysis, integrated the categories and their properties, delimited the theory, and wrote the theory. Which method is he using?
   a. constant comparative method
   b. semiotics
   c. coding
   d. memoing
   e. sorting memo

3. April spent some time in the student union listening to the discussions students had while eating lunch. She wanted to see how such discussions are socially constructed and how they vary by the social context, such as the size of the group. She was using
   a. semiotics.
   b. the constant comparative method.
   c. the Grounded Theory method.
   d. variable-oriented analysis.
   e. conversation analysis.

3. June did a study of the meanings attached to the logos on shirts and jackets. She was using
   a. elemental memos.
   b. code notes.
   c. conversation analysis.
   d. case-oriented analysis.
   e. semiotics.

4. Instead of the standardized unit of analysis in quantitative analysis, qualitative analysis uses which one of the following as the organizing principle for coding?

   a. the concept
   b. the variable
   c. the sorting memo
   d. concept mapping
   e. semiotics

5. Before doing qualitative data analysis, an important first step is to name and categorize phenomena through close examination of the data. This process is known as
   a. theoretical notes.
   b. open coding
   c. concept mapping.
   d. qualitative analysis
   e. memoing

7. Which type of notes in the memoing process deal with methodological issues?
   a. code notes
   b. theoretical notes
   c. operational notes
   d. elemental notes
   e. integrating notes

8. Tudora was nearing the end of his qualitative analysis of biker gangs. He is now at the stage where he is writing memos that tie together the various memos he has written earlier. Which type of memo is he using?
   a. elemental memo
   b. sorting memo
   c. integrating memo
   d. operational memo
   e. coding memo

9. Penelope was having difficulty seeing the relationships among the concepts in her qualitative analysis of teacher-student interactions in the classroom. She decided to put her concepts in a graphical format on a large piece of paper. She is using
   a. coding.
   b. code notes.
   c. sorting memos.
   d. the constant comparative method.
   e. concept mapping.

10. Which one of the following statements is correct?
    a. Theory is closely connected to data analysis in both quantitative and qualitative analysis.
    b. Theory is not closely connected to data analysis in either quantitative or qualitative analysis.
    c. Data collection, analysis, and theory are more intimately intertwined in quantitative analysis than in qualitative analysis.
    d. Data collection, analysis, and theory are more intimately intertwined in qualitative analysis than in quantitative analysis.
    e. None of these statements is true.

11. Professor Cessna identified how often students cheat and the severity or level of the cheating. She was looking at
    a. frequencies and structures.
    b. structures and causes.
    c. consequences and causes.
    d. processes and magnitudes.
    e. frequencies and magnitudes.

12. Cessna then looked at the different types of cheating as well as how cheating affected the student and the professor. She now was looking at
    a. frequencies and magnitudes.
    b. structures and consequences.
    c. causes and consequences.
    d. processes and causes.
    e. processes and consequences.

## DISCUSSION QUESTIONS

1. Give examples of the six different ways of looking for patterns in a particular research topic.

2. Show how a given topic of research could be analyzed differently with the two methods of cross-case analysis: variable-oriented analysis and case-oriented analysis.

3. Rewrite the four stages in the constant comparative method as used in the Grounded Theory Method.

4. Provide advice for performing qualitative data processing.

# EXERCISE 13.1 Name_____

Exercise 10.1 involved data gathering for a study of the social dynamics of jaywalking. Review your field notes if you have completed that exercise. Complete the exercise now if you have not done so before.

1. Use the strategies outlined in this chapter for processing the data. Indicate which strategies you have used and summarize the results of the data processing. Hold off with analyzing the results until the next question.

2. Use the strategies outlined in this chapter for analyzing the data. Indicate which strategies you used and summarize the results of the data analysis.

## EXERCISE 13.2                                    Name_____

Exercise 10.2 involved data gathering for a study of the social interactions among strangers. Review your field notes if you have completed that exercise. Complete the exercise now if you have not done so before.

1.  Use the strategies outlined in this chapter for processing the data. Indicate which strategies you have used and summarize the results of the data processing. Hold off with analyzing the results until the next question.

2.  Use the strategies outlined in this chapter for analyzing the data. Indicate which strategies you used and summarize the results of the data analysis.

# EXERCISE 13.3 Name_____

Use semiotics to analyze signs or symbols that strike you as having social scientific interest. Examples might include the messages and insignias on shirts and jackets, billboards, popular music, and body piercing and tatoos. You are not limited to these examples.

1. Describe specifically which symbols you studied, how many, and why you selected these symbols.

2. Use the strategies outlined in this chapter for processing the data. Indicate which strategies you have used and summarize the results of the data processing. Hold off with analyzing the results until the next question.

3. Use the strategies outlined in this chapter for analyzing the data. Indicate which strategies you used and summarize the results of the data analysis.

244

# Chapter 14

## Quantitative Data Analysis

## OBJECTIVES

1. Define quantitative analysis.

2. Describe the coding process and compare two approaches to developing code categories.

3. Offer some advice for coding a set of data.

4. Identify two functions of codebooks.

5. Present some of the common elements in codebook formats.

6. Describe several ways for entering data.

7. Define and give examples of univariate analysis.

8. Define and explain the utility of frequency distributions and marginals.

9. Explain how to calculate percentages.

10. Define central tendency.

11. Compare the mode, mean, and median in terms of calculation and interpretation.

245

12. Describe the information provided by measures of dispersion.

13. Compare the range, standard deviation, and interquartile range in terms of calculation and interpretation.

14. Distinguish continuous variables from discrete variables by definition and example.

15. Provide guidelines for balancing the demands of detail versus manageability of data presentation.

16. Differentiate the goals of univariate, bivariate, and multivariate analyses.

17. Identify the goal of subgroup comparisons.

18. Explain two techniques for handling the "don't know" response.

19. Differentiate dependent variable from independent variable by definition and example.

20. Describe how bivariate tables are presented and analyzed.

21. Explain how multivariate tables are presented and analyzed.


## SUMMARY

Quantitative analysis employs techniques whereby researchers convert data to a numerical form and subject it to statistical analysis. Quantification is the process of converting data to a numerical format, which must be in a machine-readable form so that the data can be read and manipulated by computers. The process for coding closed-ended questions is quite straightforward. Responses to open-ended questions are nonnumerical and must be coded before analysis. In the process, we reduce a wide variety of idiosyncratic items of information to a more limited set of attributes composing a variable. Remember to code as much detail as possible because code categories can later be combined if the analysis desired does not require the originally coded level of detail.

The coding scheme may already be established before the data are examined, or it may be developed after examining a number of cases to determine what set of code categories would be most appropriate. Coding choices should reflect research purposes and should reflect the logic that emerges from the data. Code categories should be both exhaustive (covering all possibilities) and mutually exclusive (no overlapping categories). It is important to verify reliability of coding procedures.

A codebook is a document that describes the locations of variables and lists the codes assigned to the attributes of the variables. It is the primary guide used in the coding process and serves as a guide for locating variables and interpreting the attributes of variables. Each variable is identified with an abbreviated name. The full definition of the variable is also reported. The codebook will also show the attributes for each variable. The codebook helps the researcher to decide which variables should be examined in which fashion.

Various options exist for converting data into a machine-readable format. Coding could be done directly on the questionnaire itself. Optical scan sheets could be used. Data entry sometimes occurs during the process of data collection, such as with computer assisted interviewing strategies. Online surveys enables respondents to enter their own data.

Social scientists perform a variety of analysis strategies on their data. There are three basic strategies: univariate analysis, bivariate analysis, and multivariate analysis. Univariate analysis involves the examination of only one variable at a time. Data are organized into frequency distributions, which are listings of the number of cases in each attribute of a variable. Each case may be listed separately, or they may be grouped in the form of marginals. Marginals sacrifice some detail in the data but provide a more manageable format for describing a distribution. In addition to raw numbers, percentages may be presented by dividing the number of cases per attribute by the base. Careful attention must be paid to determining the base, particularly in the case of missing data.

The detailed information in raw data may be simplified by calculating a measure of central tendency, a single value that summarizes a distribution. The mode reflects the attribute with the greatest frequency; the mean is calculated by summing the values and dividing by the number of cases; and the median reflects the value that cuts the distribution in half.

Measures of dispersion are calculated to reflect the spread of scores. The range is the distance between the highest and lowest values; the standard deviation reflects the difference between each score and the mean; and the interquartile range reflects the range after removing the top fourth and bottom fourth of the scores.

Which measure of dispersion or central tendency to use is determined by the nature of the data and the purpose of the analysis. For example, continuous variables and discrete variables are treated differently. Researchers sometimes violate some of the statistical assumptions, and this is legitimate to the extent that it helps interpret the data. But be aware that such procedures may lead you to think that the results represent something truly precise. Researchers are also constrained by the conflicting goals of providing complete detail versus presenting data in a manageable format.

Subgroup comparisons yield a descriptive analysis to two variables by presenting descriptive univariate data for each of several subgroups. Occasionally categories must be collapsed to enhance the analysis. "Don't know" responses can be included or excluded, depending on the purpose of the study. Subgroup comparisons focus on describing the people (or other units of analysis), and bivariate analysis focuses on the relationship between the variables themselves. Hence bivariate analysis assumes an explanatory goal.

The explanatory goal of bivariate analysis involves making causal assertions regarding a dependent variable that is at least partially determined by an independent variable. Hence bivariate analysis tables should be consistent with the logic of independent and dependent variables. Typically the attributes of the independent variable are used as column headings, and the attributes of the dependent variables are used as row headings. Percentages are then computed down (adding up to 100 percent) and compared across. But these conventions are sometimes reversed. Regardless of how a bivariate analysis is presented, it is critical to interpret such a table by comparing the independent variable subgroups with one another in terms of the attributes of the dependent variable.

Several guidelines should be followed in presenting and interpreting bivariate tables (also known as contingency tables): 1) the contents of the table should be described in a title; 2) the original content of the variables should be clearly presented in either the table itself or the text; 3) the attributes of each variable should be clearly described; 4) the base on which percentages are computed should be shown; and 5) the table should indicate the number of cases omitted from the analysis.

The logic and procedures in bivariate tabular analysis also apply to multivariate tables. But instead of explaining a dependent variable on the basis of one independent variable, such analysis explains a dependent variable on the basis of multiple independent variables. Both the separate and the combined effects of the independent variables on the dependent variable can then be examined. When the dependent variable is dichotomous, the multivariate table can be simplified by omitting the data for one attribute of the dependent variable. The two independent variables are then typically placed on the top and the side of a table, and the percentages recorded reflect one attribute of the dependent variable for each combination of attributes of the independent variables. The base for each cell should be reported.

## TERMS

1. base
2. bivariate analysis
3. central tendency
4. codebook
5. coding
6. contingency table
7. continuous variable
8. dependent variable
9. discrete variable
10. dispersion
11. frequency distribution
12. independent variable
13. interquartile range
14. marginals
15. mean
16. median
17. mode
18. multivariate analysis
19. percentages
20. quantitative analysis
21. range
22. standard deviation
23. subgroup comparisons
24. univariate analysis

## MATCHING

____ 1. The examination of the effects of two or more independent variables on a dependent variable.

____ 2. A measure of central tendency that measures the most frequent attribute.

____ 3. The measure of central tendency that is the arithmetic average.

____ 4. The measure of central tendency that divides the distribution in half.

____ 5. The measure of dispersion that resembles the standard error of a sampling distribution and that is interpreted in terms of the normal curve.

____ 6. A method of univariate analysis that simply reports the number of cases in each attribute category.

___ 7.A variable that influences another variable.

___ 8.A variable that is influenced by another variable.

## REVIEW QUESTIONS

1.  The end product of quantifying data is to convert measurements into
    a. scales.
    b. typologies.
    c. machine-readable forms.
    d. counter-sorter forms.
    e. bytes.

2.  Which one of the following is an example of a frequency distribution of grouped data for age?
    a. 18-25, 40 people; 26-50, 60 people; over 50, 20 people
    b. 18, 10 people; 19, 11 people; 20, 26 people; 21, 15 people
    c. 26, 28, 28, 30, 31, 33, 35, 41, 41, 50
    d. the mean age is 45.1
    e. the median age is 38.6

3.  Frequency distributions of grouped data are often referred to as
    a. indexicals.
    b. dispersion.
    c. epsilon.
    d. monotonicity.
    e. marginals.

4.  The process of assigning numbers to questionnaire responses is known as
    a. memoing.
    b. substitution.
    c. indexing.
    d. percentaging.
    e. coding.

5.  Which measure of central tendency divides the distribution into two halves?
    a. dispersion
    b. mode
    c. marginal
    d. median
    e. mean

6. With several extreme scores, which measure of dispersion would be most appropriate?
   a. range
   b. standard deviation
   c. standard error
   d. confidence level
   e. interquartile range

7. A fundamental dilemma in presenting data is
   a. scope versus adequacy.
   b. nominal versus ordinal values.
   c. univariate versus bivariate.
   d. detail versus manageability.
   e. variation versus central tendency.

8. Descriptive analyses are most often accomplished with which type of statistical analysis?
   a. bivariate
   b. univariate
   c. dispersion
   d. multivariate
   e. interpretation

9. Comparing the church attendance of men and women for descriptive purposes is an example of
   a. univariate analysis.
   b. multivariate analysis.
   c. subgroup comparisons.
   d. explanatory analysis.
   e. bivariate analysis.

10. Professor Dorn analyzed the relationship between age and voting behavior. This is an example of which type of analysis?
    a. univariate.
    b. bivariate.
    c. multivariate.
    d. descriptive.
    e. ex post facto.

11. The fundamental rule in reading tables is to
    a. percentage down.
    b. percentage across.
    c. read across the categories of the dependent variable in analyzing the independent variable.
    d. read across along the categories of the independent variable in analyzing the dependent variable.
    e. percentage and read in terms of the total number of cases.

12. Another term for bivariate tables is
    a. dependency tables.
    b. independency tables.
    c. marginals tables.
    d. cross-sectional tables.
    e. contingency tables.

13. Professor Goldsmid studied the relationship between gender and religiosity while controlling for social class. This is an example of which type of analysis?
    a. univariate
    b. bivariate
    c. multivariate analysis
    d. descriptive
    e. ex post facto

14. Combining two independent variables and one dependent variable into one table is possible *only* when
    a. the dependent variable is dichotomous.
    b. the independent variables are dichotomous.
    c. both the independent and dependent variables are dichotomous.
    d. a test of statistical significance is applied.
    e. a bivariate analysis is done.

## DISCUSSION QUESTIONS

1. Compare univariate and bivariate analyses in terms of definition, purpose, advantages, and limitations.

2. Compare the three measures of central tendency (mode, median, mean) in terms of definition, calculation, interpretation, and limitations.

3. Subgroup comparison is considered to be somewhat intermediate between univariate and bivariate analyses. In what sense does subgroup analysis serve a descriptive purpose, and in what sense does it serve an explanatory purpose?

4. Explain the logic in constructing and interpreting bivariate tables. Why should you percentage within categories of the independent variable and then compare across categories?

## EXERCISE 14.1                                   Name_____

You are to code the responses you got in answer to Question 7 of the questionnaire used in Exercise 9.3.

1. Code each of the responses as:
   (1) favorable to capital punishment,
   (2) unfavorable to capital punishment, or
   (3) neutral to capital punishment

          RESPONSE                              CODE (1,2,3)

1. _____            _____

2. _____            _____

3. _____            _____

4. _____            _____

5. _____            _____

6. _____            _____

7. _____            _____

8. _____            _____

9. _____            _____

10. _____            _____

2. Describe any difficulties you experienced in coding and note how you resolved them. Explain how you decided to apply codes of 1, 2, or 3.

# EXERCISE 14.2

Name_____

The number of movies attended in the preceding three months are given below for 30 people. Calculate the mean, the median, the mode, and the range. Show your work. Interpret each statistic.

| 0 | 15 | 26 | 8 | 2 |
|---|----|----|---|---|
| 3 | 11 | 13 | 0 | 3 |
| 0 | 1 | 17 | 1 | 9 |
| 7 | 4 | 18 | 12 | 10 |
| 10 | 4 | 2 | 7 | 2 |
| 2 | 5 | 9 | 6 | 6 |

1. Calculate the mean and interpret the results.

2. Calculate the median and interpret the results.

3. Calculate the mode and interpret the results.

4. Compare the three measures of central tendency you have calculated in terms of the information provided.

5. Calculate the range and interpret the results.

## EXERCISE 14.3                              Name_____

Presented below are some hypothetical data representing 50 people: (1) gender (M=male, F=female) and (2) whether they attended church last week (Y=yes, N=no).

In the steps below you will be asked to construct the appropriate bivariate percentage table showing the relationship between gender and church attendance and to give your interpretation of that table.

| | | | | | | | | | |
|---|---|---|---|---|---|---|---|---|---|
| M-N | F-N | F-Y | M-N | M-Y | F-N | F-Y | F-Y | M-N | M-Y |
| M-Y | F-Y | M-N | M-Y | F-Y | F-N | M-N | M-N | F-N | F-Y |
| M-N | F-Y | M-N | M-Y | F-Y | F-Y | M-N | M-N | F-Y | M-N |
| F-Y | M-N | M-Y | F-Y | F-N | F-Y | M-Y | F-Y | M-N | M-N |
| F-Y | F-Y | M-N | F-N | M-N | F-Y | M-N | F-Y | F-Y | M-N |

1.  Construct the bivariate percentage table appropriate for examining the relationship between sex and church attendance. Be sure to follow Babbie's suggestions for setting up a table correctly.

2.  Interpret the table. That is, compare the percentages on the independent variable in terms of the categories of the independent variable.

# EXERCISE 14.4

Name_____

Presented below is a hypothetical trivariate percentage table.

Percentage in Favor of
Gun Control

|  | Men | Women |
|---|---|---|
| Young | 50% | 70% |
| Old | 70% | 90% |

1. Explain the logical structure of the table.

2. Give your interpretation of the table.

# EXERCISE 14.5                                    Name_____

Babbie discusses the usefulness of collapsing response categories when relatively few people select extreme values on a variable. Use SPSS or MicroCase (or another data analysis program as indicated by your instructor) to apply this principle to a variable in the General Social Survey (see Appendix 1) that fits this situation: POLVIEWS. Run a frequency distribution on POLVIEWS and interpret the results. Be sure to use the "valid percent" category, which omits missing values. Then collapse the two extreme categories with the adjacent category and recalculate the percentages.

1. Report the frequency distribution before collapsing below and summarize the results.

2. Report the frequency distribution after collapsing below and summarize the results.

3. Compare the results for the two tables and note why the collapsed table may be more useful for analysis purposes.

# EXERCISE 14.6

Name_____

Select eight variables that interest you from the General Social Survey codebook in Appendix 1 of this volume. Select several items that could be used as independent variables and several that could be used as dependent variables. Use SPSS or MicroCase (or another data analysis program as indicated by your instructor) to produce frequency distributions of the variables. Request measures of central tendency.

Interpret the frequency distributions; use the "valid percent" column because it omits missing data. Interpret the appropriate statistics for five of the variables. Your interpretations should mention the level of measurement of each variable and refer only to those statistics appropriate for that level. (Note that the computer will calculate any statistics on your data whether appropriate or not.) Write your interpretations directly on the output (unless your instructor advises otherwise). Finally, write your name on the top page and list the page numbers of the printout containing your analyses.

## EXERCISE 14.7                                    Name_____

Use SPSS or MicroCase (or another data analysis program as indicated by your instructor) to construct six tables from the variables you analyzed in Exercise 14.6 involving the General Social Survey codebook contained in Appendix 1 of this volume. Select sufficient independent and dependent variables now if you have not done Exercise 14.6.

Select two tables to interpret. Be sure to 1) compare percentages on the dependent variable across categories of the independent variable, 2) summarize the relationship, and 3) briefly explain the relationship by providing possible reasons for why the relationship exists or doesn't exist. (Your task of learning how to read the tables might be more meaningful at this point if you choose variables with relatively few categories. This simplifies the structure of the tables.) Do this directly on the output (unless your instructor advises otherwise). Write your name on the top page and list the page numbers of the printout containing your analyses.

# Appendix 1

## General Social Survey

The General Social Survey (GSS) is a survey done by the National Opinion Research Center on the attitudes, behaviors, and background characteristics of the American population. These surveys have occurred almost annually since 1972 and typically involve samples of about 1500 Americans 18 years old or older. Samples are full probability samples, and the samples reflect multistage area probability samples to the block level. The primary sampling units employed are Standard Metropolitan Statistical Areas or nonmetropolitan counties, stratified by region, age, and race before selection. The units of selection at the second stage are block groups and enumeration districts, which were stratified according to race and income before selection. The third stage of selection involves blocks, which were selected with probabilities proportional to size.

The data file you will be using contains random samples of 500 cases for each of the years of 1978, 1983, 1988, 1993, and 1998, resulting in a total sample of 2,500 cases. You may wish to limit your analyses to only one year, do separate analyses for various years, or combine various years in one analysis. Unless you specifically select certain years, your analyses will include data from all years. Be very clear on which subgroups you will use in your analysis. If you use the full sample of 2,500 cases across all years to study attitudes toward abortion, for example, changes that occurred in attitudes over the years will not be evident and may even mask relationships you wish to examine between, say, gender and attitudes toward abortion. That is, if women were more likely support abortion in the early years and men in the later years, a table relating gender to abortion support for the entire sample would show few gender differences. Also, some items were not asked at each of the years in the data set. If you see a relatively high number of "system missing" responses for an item, that item probably was not asked at each of the years in the data set.

Be sure you distinguish clearly between independent and dependent variables in your analyses. Many of the typically independent variables, such as gender, age, and race, are located toward the beginning of the data file. Some variables, such as how much people watch TV or their level of education, could be either independent or dependent. Select an appropriate number of what you consider independent and dependent variables, or as many of each type as indicated by your instructor.

| | | |
|---|---|---|
| **YEAR** | 1. | Year of sample. |
| | | 78, 83, 88, 93, or 98 |
| | | |
| **ID** | 2. | Case ID |
| | | ID number |

**REGION**   3.   Region of interview.
1.   New England
2.   Middle Atlantic
3.   East North Central
4.   West North Central
5.   South Atlantic
6.   East South Central
7.   West South Central
8.   Mountain
9.   Pacific

**SIZE**   4.   Size of place of interview in 1000s (i.e., add three zeroes).
0.   Less than 1,000

**SIZE3**   5.   SIZE variable recoded into thirds.
1.   Small
2.   Moderate
3.   Large

**RACE**   6.   What race do you consider yourself?
1.   White
2.   Black
3.   Other

**SEX**   7.   Sex (coded by interviewer).
1.   Male
2.   Female

**AGE**            8.  Age (determined by asking date of birth, actual ages recorded).
                  0.  Missing
             99.  Missing, no answer

**AGE3**           9.  AGE variable recoded into thirds.
                  1.  18-32
                  2.  33-51
                  3.  52-89

**MARITAL**        10.  Are you currently married, widowed, divorced, separated, or have you never been married?
                  1.  Married
                  2.  Widowed
                  3.  Divorced
                  4.  Separated
                  5.  Never married
                  9.  Missing

**DEGREE**         11.  Highest degree.
                  0.  Less than high school
                  1.  High school
                  2.  Associate/junior college
                  3.  Bachelor's
                  4.  Graduate
                  7.  Missing, not applicable
                  8.  Missing, don't know
                  9.  Missing, no answer

**EDUC**           12.  Highest year of school completed.
             0-19.  Actual number of years
              20.  20 or more (i.e., 8 years of college or more)
              98.  Missing, don't know
              99.  Missing, no answer

**EDUC3**          13.  EDUC variable recoded into thirds.
                  1.  less than high school graduation
                  2.  high school graduation
                  3.  more than high school graduation

**INCOME**    14. In which of the following groups did your total *family* income, from *all* sources, fall last year before taxes, that is?
1. Under $1,000
2. $1,000 to 2,999
3. $3,000 to 3,999
4. $4,000 to 4,999
5. $5,000 to 5,999
6. $6,000 to 6,999
7. $7,000 to 7,999
8. $8,000 to 9,999
9. $10,000 to 14,999
10. $15,000 to 19,999
11. $20,000 to 24,999
12. $25,000 or over
13. Refused (treat as missing, unless you wish to study them)
98. Missing, don't know
99. Missing, no answer

**REALINC**    15. Family income in constant dollars ($1 thru $999,997).

**REALINC3**    16. REALINC variable recoded into thirds.
1. Low
2. Moderate
3. High

**PRESTIGE**    17. Hodge/Siegel/Rossi prestige scale score for respondent's occupation (actual score recorded).

**PRESTIG3**    18. PRESTIGE variable recoded into thirds.
1. Low
2. Moderate
3. High

**PAPRES16**    19. Hodge/Siegel/Rossi prestige scale score for father's occupation when respondent was growing up (actual score recorded).

**PAPRES3**    20. PAPRES16 variable recoded into thirds.
1. Low
2. Moderate
3. High

**RELIG** 21. What is your religious preference? Is it Protestant, Catholic, Jewish, some other religion, or no religion?
 1. Protestant
 2. Catholic
 3. Jewish
 4. None
 5. Other
 8. Missing, don't know
 9. Missing, no answer

**ATTEND** 22. How often do you attend religious services?
 0. Never
 1. Less than once a year
 2. About once or twice a year
 3. Several times a year
 4. About once a month
 5. 2-3 times a month
 6. Nearly every week
 7. Every week
 8. Several times a week
 9. Missing

**CHILDS** 23. How many children have you ever had? Please count all that were born alive at any time (including any you had from a previous marriage).
 0-7. Actual number (e.g., 3 means 3 children)
 8. Eight or more
 9. Missing

**SIBS** 24. How many brothers and sisters did you have? Please count those born alive, but no longer living, as well as those alive now. Also include stepbrothers and stepsisters, and children adopted by your parents (actual number recorded).
 98. Missing, don't know
 99. Missing, no answer

**SIBS3** 25. SIBS variable recoded into thirds.
 1. 0-2
 2. 3-4
 3. 5 or more

**PARTYID**   26.   Generally speaking, do you usually think of yourself as a Republican, Democrat, Independent, or what?
0.   Strong Democrat
1.   Not very strong Democrat
2.   Independent, close to Democrat
3.   Independent (neither, no response)
4.   Independent, close to Republican
5.   Not very strong Republican
6.   Strong Republican
7.   Other party, refused to say
9.   Missing, no answer

**POLVIEWS**   27.   I'm going to show you a seven-point scale on which the political views that people might hold are arranged from extremely liberal—point 1—to extremely conservative—point 7. Where would you place yourself on this scale?
1.   Extremely liberal
2.   Liberal
3.   Slightly liberal
4.   Moderate, middle of the road
5.   Slightly conservative
6.   Conservative
7.   Extremely conservative
8.   Missing, don't know
9.   Missing, no answer

**ZODIAC**   28.   Astrological sign of respondent.

| 1. Aries | 8. Scorpio |
|---|---|
| 2. Taurus | 9. Sagittarius |
| 3. Gemini | 10. Capricorn |
| 4. Cancer | 11. Aquarius |
| 5. Leo | 12. Pisces |
| 6. Virgo | 99. Missing |
| 7. Libra | |

**TVHOURS**   29.   On the average day, about how many hours do you personally watch television (actual number of hours recorded)?
98.   Missing, don't know
99.   Missing, no answer

**TVHOURS3**    30. TVHOURS variable recoded into thirds.
  1. 0-1
  2. 2-3
  3. 4-24

**OWNGUN**    31. Do you happen to have in your home any guns or revolvers?
  1. Yes
  2. No
  3. Refused
  9. Missing, no answer

**MEMNUM**    32. Number of groups or organizations to which respondent belongs (actual number recorded).
  98. Missing, don't know
  99. Missing, no answer

**MEMNUM3**    33. MEMNUM variable recoded into thirds.
  0. Zero
  1. One
  2. Two or more

**FINRELA**    34. Compared with American families in general, would you say your family income is far below average, below average, average, above average, or far above average?
  1. Far below average
  2. Below average
  3. Average
  4. Above average
  5. Far above average
  8. Missing, don't know
  9. Missing, no answer

**MAWORK**    35. Did your mother ever work for pay for as long as a year, after she was married?
  1. Yes
  2. No
  8. Missing, don't know
  9. Missing, no answer

**POSTLIFE**      36.  Do you believe there is a life after death?
                       1.  Yes
                       2.  No
                       8.  Missing, don't know
                       9.  Missing, no answer

Please tell me whether or not *you* think it should be possible for a pregnant woman to obtain a *legal* abortion if. . .(applies to items 37-42)

**ABANY**         37.  The woman wants it for any reason?
                       1.  Yes
                       2.  No
                       8.  Missing, don't know
                       9.  Missing, no answer

**ABDEFECT**      38.  If there is a strong chance of serious defect in the baby?
                       (same answers as ABANY, #37)

**ABHLTH**        39.  If the woman's own health is seriously endangered by the pregnancy?
                       (same answer as ABANY, #37)

**ABPOOR**        40.  If the family has a very low income and cannot afford any more children?
                       (same answers as ABANY, #37)

**ABRAPE**        41.  If she became pregnant as a result of rape?
                       (same answers as ABANY, #37)

**ABSINGLE**      42.  If she is not married and does not want to marry the man?
                       (same answers as ABANY, #37)

**AGED**          43.  As you know, many older people share a home with their grown children. Do you think this is generally a good idea or a bad idea?
                       1.  A good idea
                       2.  Bad idea
                       3.  Depends
                       8.  Missing, don't know
                       9.  Missing, no answer

Now I'd like your opinions on a number of different things. Some people agree with a statement, others disagree. As I read each one, tell me whether you more or less agree with it, or more or less disagree (applies to items 44-46).

ANOMIA5    44. In spite of what some people say, the lot (situation/condition) of the average man is getting worse, not better.
1. Agree
2. Disagree
8. Missing, don't know
9. Missing, no answer

ANOMIA6    45. It's hardly fair to bring a child into the world with the way things look for the future.
(same answers as ANOMIA5, #44)

ANOMIA7    46. Most public officials (people in public office) are not really interested in the problems of the average man.
(same answers as ANOMIA5, #44)

CAPPUN    47. Do you favor or oppose the death penalty for persons convicted of murder?
1. Favor
2. Oppose
8. Missing, don't know
9. Missing, no answer

I am going to name some institutions in this country. As far as the *people running* these institutions are concerned, would you say you have a great deal of confidence, only some confidence, or hardly any confidence at all in them (applies to items 48-50)?

CONEDUC    48. Education?
1. A great deal
2. Only some
3. Hardly any
8. Missing, don't know
9. Missing, no answer

CONLEGIS    49. Congress?
(same answers as CONEDUC, #48)

**CONPRESS**    50.  Press?
                     (same answers as CONEDUC, #48)

**COURTS**      51.  In general, do you think the courts in this area deal too harshly
                     or not harshly enough with criminals?
                     1.   Too harshly
                     2.   Not harshly enough
                     3.   About right (volunteered)
                     8.   Missing, don't know
                     9.   Missing, no answer

**GRASS**       52.  Do you think the use of marijuana should be made legal or not?
                     1.   Should be made legal
                     2.   Should not be made legal
                     8.   Missing, don't know
                     9.   Missing, no answer

**HAPPY**       53.  Taken all together, how would you say things are these days—
                     would you say that you are very happy, pretty happy, or not too
                     happy?
                     1.   Very happy
                     2.   Pretty happy
                     3.   Not too happy
                     8.   Missing, don't know
                     9.   Missing, no answer

**HELPFUL**     54.  Would you say that most of the time people try to be helpful, or
                     that they are mostly just looking out for themselves?
                     1.   Try to be helpful
                     2.   Just look out for themselves
                     3.   Depends (volunteered)
                     8.   Missing, don't know
                     9.   Missing, no answer

**HIT**         55.  Have you ever been punched or beaten by another person?
                     1.   Yes
                     2.   No
                     8.   Missing, don't know
                     9.   Missing, no answer

**HITOK**     56.  Are there any situations that you can imagine in which you would would approve of a man punching an adult male stranger?
  1.  Yes
  2.  No
  8.  Missing, don't know
  9.  Missing, no answer

We are faced with many problems in this country, none of which can be solved easily or inexpensively. I'm going to name some of these problems, and for each one I'd like you to tell me whether you think we're spending too much money on it, too little money, or about the right amount. Are we spending too much, too little, or about the right amount on. . .(applies to items 57-61)

**NATCRIME**  57.  Halting the rising crime rate?
  1.  Too little
  2.  About right
  3.  Too much
  8.  Missing, don't know
  9.  Missing, no answer

**NATDRUG**   58.  Dealing with drug addiction?
          (same answers as NATCRIME, #57)

**NATEDUC**   59.  Improving the nation's education system?
          (same answers as NATCRIME, #57)

**NATENVIR**  60.  Improving and protecting the environment?
          (same answers as NATCRIME, #57)

**NATFARE**   61.  Welfare?
          (same answers as NATCRIME, #57)

**POLHITOK**  62.  Are there any situations you can imagine in which you would approve of a policeman striking an adult male citizen?
  1.  Yes
  2.  No
  8.  Not sure
  9.  Missing, no answer

The next questions are about pornography—books, movies, magazines, and photographs that show or describe sex activities. I'm going to read some opinions about the effects of looking at or reading such sexual materials. As I read each one, please tell me if you think sexual materials do or do not have that effect (applies to items 63-65).

**PORNINF**     63.   Sexual materials provide information about sex?
                      1.   Yes
                      2.   No
                      8.   Missing, don't know
                      9.   Missing, no answer

**PORNOUT**     64.   Sexual materials provide an outlet for bottled-up impulses?
                      (same answers as PORNINF, #63)

**PORNRAPE**    65.   Sexual materials lead people to commit rape?
                      (same answers as PORNINF, #63)

**RACLIVE**     66.   Are there any (Negroes/Blacks) living in this neighborhood now?
                      1.   Yes
                      2.   No
                      8.   Missing, don't know
                      9.   Missing, no answer

**SATCITY**     67.   How much satisfaction do you get from the city or place you live in?
                      1.   A very great deal
                      2.   A great deal
                      3.   Quite a bit
                      4.   A fair amount
                      5.   Some
                      6.   A little
                      7.   None
                      8.   Missing, don't know
                      9.   Missing, no answer

**SATFAM**      68.   How much satisfaction do you get from your family life?
                      (same answers as SATCITY, #67)

**SATFRND**       69. How much satisfaction do you get from your friendships? (same answers as SATCITY, #67)

**SATHEALT**      70. How much satisfaction do you get from your health and physical condition?   (same answers as SATCITY, #67)

**SATFIN**        71. We are interested in how people are getting along financially these days. So far as you and your family are concerned, would you say that you are pretty well satisfied with your present financial situation, more or less satisfied, or not satisfied at all?
   1. Pretty well satisfied
   2. More or less satisfied
   3. Not satisfied at all
   8. Missing, don't know
   9. Missing, no answer

# Appendix 2

## Answers to Matching and Review Questions

Number in parentheses is the page number where answer is found.

CHAPTER 1

| Matching | | | Review Questions | | | | | | |
|---|---|---|---|---|---|---|---|---|---|
| 1. | 17 | (5) | 1. | d | (3) | 9. | d | (19) |
| 2. | 19 | (18) | 2. | d | (4) | 10. | e | (10) |
| 3. | 4 | (6) | 3. | b | (10) | 11. | a | (12) |
| 4. | 20 | (6) | 4. | d | (5) | 12. | b | (14) |
| 5. | 29 | (7) | 5. | c | (6) | 13. | e | (15) |
| 6. | 30 | (12) | 6. | b | (7) | 14. | b | (16) |
| 7. | 34 | (14) | 7. | d | (8) | | | |
| 8. | 28 | (15) | 8. | a | (7) | | | |

CHAPTER 2

| Matching | | | Review Questions | | | | | | |
|---|---|---|---|---|---|---|---|---|---|
| 1. | 11 | (36) | 1. | d | (32) | 9. | a | (37) |
| 2. | 8 | (46) | 2. | a | (36) | 10. | c | (46) |
| 3. | 14 | (30) | 3. | a | (36) | 11. | b | (31) |
| 4. | 4 | (32) | 4. | d | (28) | 12. | e | (44) |
| 5. | 3 | (31) | 5. | b | (46) | 13. | b | (46) |
| 6. | 2 | (38) | 6. | a | (36) | | | |
| 7. | 12 | (27) | 7. | c | (29) | | | |
| 8. | 13 | (31) | 8. | e | (30) | | | |

## CHAPTER 3

Matching

| | | |
|---|---|---|
| 1. | 8 | (56) |
| 2. | 1 | (58) |
| 3. | 3 | (58) |
| 4. | 2 | (65) |
| 5. | 7 | (69) |
| 6. | 6 | (71) |

Review Questions

| | | | | | |
|---|---|---|---|---|---|
| 1. | e | (55) | 8. | c | (65) |
| 2. | e | (55) | 9. | a | (63) |
| 3. | b | (56) | 10. | a | (68) |
| 4. | d | (56) | 11. | b | (69) |
| 5. | b | (58) | 12. | c | (71) |
| 6. | a | (68) | | | |
| 7. | c | (65) | | | |

## CHAPTER 4

Matching

| | | |
|---|---|---|
| 1. | 12 | (96) |
| 2. | 5 | (85) |
| 3. | 17 | (89) |
| 4. | 4 | (95) |
| 5. | 6 | (83) |
| 6. | 2 | (96) |
| 7. | 1 | (98) |
| 8. | 11 | (98) |

Review Questions

| | | | | | |
|---|---|---|---|---|---|
| 1. | c | (83) | 9. | d | (94) |
| 2. | c | (85) | 10. | e | (97) |
| 3. | c | (83) | 11. | d | (97) |
| 4. | a | (85) | 12. | e | (98) |
| 5. | d | (84) | 13. | c | (99) |
| 6. | d | (95) | 14. | b | (107) |
| 7. | a | (90) | 15. | d | (85) |
| 8. | b | (91) | 16. | b | (86) |

## CHAPTER 5

Matching

| | | |
|---|---|---|
| 1. | 17 | (115) |
| 2. | 4 | (118) |
| 3. | 13 | (118) |
| 4. | 19 | (120) |
| 5. | 21 | (120) |
| 6. | 27 | (136) |
| 7. | 30 | (139) |
| 8. | 28 | (138) |

Review Questions

| | | | | | |
|---|---|---|---|---|---|
| 1. | a | (116) | 10. | d | (129) |
| 2. | b | (118) | 11. | e | (130) |
| 3. | e | (128) | 12. | c | (131) |
| 4. | a | (118) | 13. | c | (136) |
| 5. | d | (119) | 14. | c | (136) |
| 6. | e | (117) | 15. | c | (139) |
| 7. | a | (127) | 16. | a | (140) |
| 8. | b | (120) | 17. | d | (140) |
| 9. | a | (124) | | | |

## CHAPTER 6

Matching

1.  8    (147)
2.  14   (147)
3.  6    (149)
4.  19   (150)
5.  11   (159)
6.  5    (160)
7.  12   (164)
8.  18   (169)

Review Questions

1.  d   (147)      9.   e   (164)
2.  b   (147)     10    a   (165)
3.  c   (147)     11.   d   (164)
4.  b   (149)     12.   b   (166)
5.  e   (150)     13.   e   (169)
6.  c   (154)     14.   c   (170)
7.  a   (156)
8.  c   (159)

## CHAPTER 7

Matching

1.  6    (184)
2.  13   (184)
3.  29   (179)
4.  30   (188)
5.  28   (197)
6.  33   (197)
7.  31   (200)
8.  1    (178)

Review Questions

1.  d   (175)      9.   d   (186)
2.  b   (176)     10.   e   (187)
3.  d   (179)     11.   a   (192)
4.  b   (179)     12.   a   (197)
5.  c   (181)     13.   d   (198)
6.  b   (184)     14.   c   (200)
7.  c   (194)     15.   a   (203)
8.  a   (196)     16.   e   (208)

## CHAPTER 8

Matching

1.  4    (219)
2.  1    (219)
3.  25   (222)
4.  22   (224)
5.  3    (221)
6.  13   (225)
7.  15   (225)
8.  10   (225)

Review Questions

1.  e   (218)      9.   b   (225)
2.  c   (228)     10.   e   (226)
3.  a   (219)     11.   b   (225)
4.  c   (219)     12.   d   (227)
5.  a   (230)     13.   b   (228)
6.  c   (219)     14.   d   (229)
7.  c   (221)     15.   a   (233)
8.  c   (223)

## CHAPTER 9

### Matching

1.  19   (247)
2.  16   (259)
3.   8   (273)
4.  17   (258)
5.   9   (243)
6.  20   (265)
7.  13   (264)
8.  18   (273)

### Review Questions

| | | | | | |
|---|---|---|---|---|---|
| 1. | d | (242) | 9. | d | (257) |
| 2. | a | (243) | 10. | d | (258) |
| 3. | e | (243) | 11. | c | (259) |
| 4. | c | (246) | 12. | d | (262) |
| 5. | a | (247) | 13. | a | (265) |
| 6. | d | (248) | 14. | d | (266) |
| 7. | a | (248) | 15. | c | (274) |
| 8. | a | (250) | | | |

## CHAPTER 10

### Matching

1.   4   (288)
2.   8   (288)
3.   6   (290)
4.   1   (291)
5.   2   (292)
6.   7   (293)
7.  11   (294)
8.   5   (300)

### Review Questions

| | | | | | |
|---|---|---|---|---|---|
| 1. | b | (281) | 9. | c | (302) |
| 2. | b | (288) | 10. | c | (282) |
| 3. | e | (288) | 11. | a | (293) |
| 4. | d | (290) | 12. | a | (294) |
| 5. | b | (282) | 13. | b | (305) |
| 6. | a | (284) | | | |
| 7. | e | (296) | | | |
| 8. | d | (297) | | | |

## CHAPTER 11

### Matching

1.   4   (312)
2.  10   (317)
3.   9   (317)
4.   6   (325)
5.   5   (333)
6.  11   (311)
7.  12   (334)
8.   8   (334)

### Review Questions

| | | | | | |
|---|---|---|---|---|---|
| 1. | b | (312) | 9. | b | (325) |
| 2. | e | (313) | 10. | c | (325) |
| 3. | e | (316) | 11. | e | (325) |
| 4. | c | (317) | 12. | d | (325) |
| 5. | e | (317) | 13. | a | (327) |
| 6. | e | (322) | 14. | b | (334) |
| 7. | d | (323) | | | |
| 8. | a | (324) | | | |

## CHAPTER 12

| Matching | | |
|---|---|---|
| 1. | 9 | (348) |
| 2. | 8 | (344) |
| 3. | 7 | (350) |
| 4. | 11 | (361) |
| 5. | 13 | (358) |
| 6. | 4 | (342) |
| 7. | 1 | (342) |
| 8. | 5 | (345) |

| Review Questions | | | | | |
|---|---|---|---|---|---|
| 1. | e | (341) | 9. | c | (348) |
| 2. | b | (342) | 10. | b | (350) |
| 3. | c | (341) | 11. | c | (346) |
| 4. | d | (345) | 12. | a | (353) |
| 5. | b | (346) | 13. | d | (355) |
| 6. | e | (345) | 14. | e | (362) |
| 7. | c | (346) | | | |
| 8. | d | (348) | | | |

## CHAPTER 13

| Matching | | |
|---|---|---|
| 1. | 18 | (370) |
| 2. | 9 | (371) |
| 3. | 3 | (375) |
| 4. | 17 | (379) |
| 5. | 16 | (380) |
| 6. | 4 | (380) |
| 7. | 14 | (369) |
| 8. | 1 | (371) |

| Review Questions | | | | | |
|---|---|---|---|---|---|
| 1. | d | (371) | 9. | e | (380) |
| 2. | a | (371) | 10. | d | (370) |
| 3. | e | (374) | 11. | e | (370) |
| 4. | e | (372) | 12. | b | (370) |
| 5. | a | (376) | | | |
| 6. | b | (376) | | | |
| 7. | c | (379) | | | |
| 8. | c | (380) | | | |

## CHAPTER 14

| Matching | | |
|---|---|---|
| 1. | 18 | (415) |
| 2. | 17 | (402) |
| 3. | 15 | (402) |
| 4. | 16 | (402) |
| 5. | 22 | (405) |
| 6. | 11 | (401) |
| 7. | 12 | (410) |
| 8. | 8 | (410) |

| Review Questions | | | | | |
|---|---|---|---|---|---|
| 1. | c | (395) | 9. | c | (406) |
| 2. | a | (403) | 10. | b | (410) |
| 3. | e | (402) | 11. | d | (411) |
| 4. | e | (396) | 12. | e | (414) |
| 5. | d | (402) | 13. | c | (415) |
| 6. | e | (405) | 14. | a | (416) |
| 7. | d | (406) | | | |
| 8. | b | (400) | | | |